Review the CFAT!

Complete Canadian Forces Aptitude Test Study Guide And Practice Test Questions

Published by

Complete TEST
Preparation Inc.

Copyright

The Canadian Armed Forces is not involved in the production of, and does not endorse this publication.

We strongly recommend that students check with exam providers for up-to-date information regarding test content.

Version 6.6 January 2016

ISBN: 9781928077053

Published by
Complete Test Preparation Inc.
Visit us on the web at http://www.test-preparation.ca
Printed in the USA

About Complete Test Preparation Inc.

The Complete Test Preparation Inc. Team has been publishing high quality study materials since 2005. Thousands of students visit our websites every year, and thousands of students, teachers and parents all over the world have purchased our teaching materials, curriculum, study guides and practice tests.

Complete Test Preparation Inc. is committed to provide students with the best study materials and practice tests available on the market. Members of our team combine years of teaching experience, with experienced writers and editors, all with advanced degrees.

Feedback

We welcome your feedback. Email us at feedback@test-preparation.ca with your comments and suggestions. We carefully review all suggestions and often incorporate reader suggestions into upcoming versions. As a Print on Demand Publisher, we update our products frequently.

Contents

7   **Getting Started**
How this Study Guide is Organized   8

9   **Verbal Skills (VS)**
Verbal Skills Self-Assessment   11
Answer Key   22
Help with Building your Vocabulary   25
How to Answer Verbal Analogies   28

31   **Problem Solving (PS)**
Problem Solving Self-Assessment   36
Answer Key   44
Types of Arithmetic Reasoning Problems   51
Sequences Tutorial   59
Types of Number Sequence Problems   60
Strategy for Answering Sequence Questions   63

64   **Spatial Ability (SA)**
Spatial Ability Self-Assessment   67
Answer Key   71

72   **Practice Test Questions Set 1**
Answer Key   96

104   **Practice Test Questions Set 2**
Answer Key   129

136   **Conclusion**

Getting Started

CONGRATULATIONS! By deciding to take the Canadian Forces Aptitude Test (CFAT), you have taken the first step toward a great future! Of course, there is no point in taking this important examination unless you intend to do your very best to earn the highest grade you possibly can. That means getting yourself organized and discovering the best approaches, methods and strategies to master the material. Yes, that will require real effort and dedication on your part but if you are willing to focus your energy and devote the study time necessary, before you know it you will be opening that letter of acceptance to the Canadian Armed Services.

We know that taking on a new endeavour can be a little scary, and it is easy to feel unsure of where to begin. That's where we come in. This study guide is designed to help you improve your test-taking skills, show you a few tricks of the trade and increase both your competency and confidence.

The Canadian Armed Forces Aptitude Test

The CFAT has 3 sections, Verbal Skills, including basic vocabulary and verbal analogies, Spatial Ability, where you are asked to recognize shapes and patterns, and Problem Solving, which includes, word problems (arithmetic reasoning), sequences and non-verbal reasoning problems, where you are asked to recognize shapes after some transformation, for example, rotation.

While we seek to make our guide as comprehensive as possible, note that like all entrance exams, the CFAT Exam might be adjusted at some future point. New material might be added, or content that is no longer relevant or applicable might be removed. It is always a good idea to give the materials you receive when you register to take the CFAT a careful review.

How this Study Guide is Organized

This study guide has three components. The first section, Self-Assessments, will help you recognize your areas of strength and weaknesses. This will be a boon when it comes to managing your study time most efficiently; there is not much point of focusing on material you have already got firmly under control. Instead, taking the self-assessments will show you where that time could be much better spent. In this area you will begin with a few questions to evaluate quickly your understanding of material that is likely to appear on the CFAT. If you do poorly in certain areas, simply work carefully through those sections in the tutorials and then try the self-assessment again.

The second component, Tutorials, offers information in each of the content areas, as well as strategies to help you master that material. The tutorials are not intended to be a complete course, but cover general principles. If you find that you do not understand the tutorials, it is recommended that you seek out additional instruction.

Third, we offer two sets of practice test questions, similar to those on the CFAT Exam.

Verbal Skills (VS)

THIS SECTION CONTAINS A SELF-ASSESSMENT AND VERBAL SKILLS TUTORIAL. The tutorials are designed to familiarize general principles and the self-assessment contains general questions similar to the verbal skills questions likely to be on the CFAT exam, but are not intended to be identical to the exam questions. If you do not understand parts of the tutorial, or find the tutorial difficult, it is recommended that you seek out additional instruction.

Tour of the Verbal Skills Content

First, lets look at what verbal skills are. Verbal skills on the CFAT are really just another name for vocabulary and analogies questions. The CFAT has four different types of verbal skills questions: synonyms, where you are required to choose a word with the same meaning, antonyms, where you are required to choose a word with the opposite meaning, and definition questions, where you are required to choose the definition of a given word. Lets review vocabulary first.

Here are examples of the three types of vocabulary questions.

1. Synonym example:

HOUSE means the same as

    a. Farm

    b. Residence

    c. Office

    d. Building

The answer is B, since residence and house are synonyms.

2. Antonym example:

SPEED is the opposite of

   a. Slow
   b. Quick
   c. Tardy
   d. Lazy

The answer is A. Slow and Speed are opposites.

3. Definition example:

AQUATIC animals live

   a. In trees
   b. On land
   c. Underwater
   d. In mountains

The answer is C. Aquatic means of, or relating to water.

The fourth type of question in the verbal skills section is
verbal analogies. Verbal analogies questions give one pair
of related words, and another word without its pair. You
are asked to find a word that has the same relationship as
the given pair. A variation on this style is you are given a
pair and must choose a word pair with the same relationship from a list of pairs.

4. Verbal analogy example:

Writing : publishing   cooking: _____

   a. baking
   b. eating
   c. cleaning
   d. washing

Answer: B
This is a steps-in-a-process relationship. You have to

write before publishing in the same way that you have to cook before eating. Note that you can of course, eat without cooking but that is not an option in this question.

Verbal Skills Self-Assessment

The purpose of the self-assessment is:

- Identify your strengths and weaknesses.

- Get accustomed to the CFAT format

- Extra practice – the self-assessments are almost a full 3rd practice test!

- Provide a baseline score in the verbal skills section

Since this is a self-assessment, and depending on how confident you are with verbal skills, timing is optional. The CFAT has 15 verbal skills questions to be completed in 5 minutes. The self-assessment has 40 questions, so allow about 20 minutes to complete this assessment.

The self-assessment is designed to give you a baseline score in the different areas covered. Here is a brief outline of how your score on the self-assessment relates to your understanding of the material.

75% - 100%	Excellent – you have mastered the content.
50 – 75%	Good. You have a working knowledge. Even though you can just pass this section, you may want to review the tutorials and do some extra practice to see if you can improve your mark.
25% - 50%	Below Average. You do not understand the problems. Review the tutorials, and retake this quiz again in a few days, before proceeding to the rest of the study guide.

Less than 25%	Poor. You have a very limited under-standing of the problems. Please review the tutorials, and retake this quiz again in a few days, before proceeding to the rest of the study guide.

The questions below are not the same as you will find on the CFAT - that would be too easy! And nobody knows what the questions will be and they change all the time. Below are general verbal skills questions. So, while the format and exact wording of the questions may differ slightly, and change from year to year, if you can answer the questions below, you will have no problem with the verbal skills section of the CFAT.

After taking the Self-Assessment, use the table above to assess your understanding. If you scored low, read through the tutorials and try again in a few days.

Verbal Skills Self-Assessment Answer Sheet

1. Ⓐ Ⓑ Ⓒ Ⓓ   21. Ⓐ Ⓑ Ⓒ Ⓓ

2. Ⓐ Ⓑ Ⓒ Ⓓ   22. Ⓐ Ⓑ Ⓒ Ⓓ

3. Ⓐ Ⓑ Ⓒ Ⓓ   23. Ⓐ Ⓑ Ⓒ Ⓓ

4. Ⓐ Ⓑ Ⓒ Ⓓ   24. Ⓐ Ⓑ Ⓒ Ⓓ

5. Ⓐ Ⓑ Ⓒ Ⓓ   25. Ⓐ Ⓑ Ⓒ Ⓓ

6. Ⓐ Ⓑ Ⓒ Ⓓ   26. Ⓐ Ⓑ Ⓒ Ⓓ

7. Ⓐ Ⓑ Ⓒ Ⓓ   27. Ⓐ Ⓑ Ⓒ Ⓓ

8. Ⓐ Ⓑ Ⓒ Ⓓ   28. Ⓐ Ⓑ Ⓒ Ⓓ

9. Ⓐ Ⓑ Ⓒ Ⓓ   29. Ⓐ Ⓑ Ⓒ Ⓓ

10. Ⓐ Ⓑ Ⓒ Ⓓ   30. Ⓐ Ⓑ Ⓒ Ⓓ

11. Ⓐ Ⓑ Ⓒ Ⓓ   31. Ⓐ Ⓑ Ⓒ Ⓓ

12. Ⓐ Ⓑ Ⓒ Ⓓ   32. Ⓐ Ⓑ Ⓒ Ⓓ

13. Ⓐ Ⓑ Ⓒ Ⓓ   33. Ⓐ Ⓑ Ⓒ Ⓓ

14. Ⓐ Ⓑ Ⓒ Ⓓ   34. Ⓐ Ⓑ Ⓒ Ⓓ

15. Ⓐ Ⓑ Ⓒ Ⓓ   35. Ⓐ Ⓑ Ⓒ Ⓓ

16. Ⓐ Ⓑ Ⓒ Ⓓ   36. Ⓐ Ⓑ Ⓒ Ⓓ

17. Ⓐ Ⓑ Ⓒ Ⓓ   37. Ⓐ Ⓑ Ⓒ Ⓓ

18. Ⓐ Ⓑ Ⓒ Ⓓ   38. Ⓐ Ⓑ Ⓒ Ⓓ

19. Ⓐ Ⓑ Ⓒ Ⓓ   39. Ⓐ Ⓑ Ⓒ Ⓓ

20. Ⓐ Ⓑ Ⓒ Ⓓ   40. Ⓐ Ⓑ Ⓒ Ⓓ

1. PETAL is to FLOWER as FUR is to

    a. Coat

    b. Warm

    c. Woman

    d. Rabbit

2. PRESENT is to BIRTHDAY as REWARD is to

    a. Accomplishment

    b. Medal

    c. Acceptance

    d. Cash

3. SHOVEL is to DIG as SCISSORS is to

    a. Scoop

    b. Carry

    c. Snip

    d. Rip

4. FINGER is to HAND as LEG is to

    a. Body

    b. Foot

    c. Toe

    d. Hip

5. SLEEP IN is to LATE as SKIP BREAKFAST is to

    a. Hungry

    b. Early

    c. Lunch

    d. dinner

6. CIRCLE is to SPHERE as SQUARE is to

    a. Triangle

    b. Oval

    c. Half Circle

    d. Cube

7. ORANGE is to FRUIT as CARROT is to

    a. Vegetable

    b. Bean

    c. Food

    d. Apple

8. PAPER is to LIGHT as LEAD is to

    a. Grey

    b. Solid

    c. Thick

    d. Heavy

9. STEEL is to CAR as GLASS is to

    a. Pane

    b. Window

    c. Transparent

    d. Fragile

10. FOUR-LEAF CLOVER is to LUCK as CROSS is to

    a. Christianity

    b. Religion

    c. Wood

    d. Tree

11. CONSPICUOUS means the same as

    a. Important

    b. Prominent

    c. Beautiful

    d. Convincing

12. BENEVOLENCE means the same as

    a. Happiness

    b. Courage

    c. Kindness

    d. Loyalty

13. BOISTEROUS means the same as

    a. Loud

    b. Soft

    c. Gentle

    d. Warm

14. FONDLE means the same as

    a. Hold

    b. Caress

    c. Throw

    d. Keep

15. MOMENTOUS means the same as

    a. Magical

    b. Interesting

    c. Imaginary

    d. Very important

16. ANTAGONIST means the same as

    a. Supporter

    b. Fan

    c. Enemy

    d. Partner

17. MEMENTO means the same as

    a. Monument

    b. Gift

    c. Reminder

    d. Idea

18. INSIDIOUS means the same as

    a. Wise

    b. Brave

    c. Helpful

    d. Gradual

19. ITINERARY means the same as

    a. Schedule

    b. Guidebook

    c. Pass

    d. Diary

20. ILLUSTRIOUS means the same as

    a. Rich

    b. Noble

    c. Gallant

    d. Poor

21. AUTHENTIC is the opposite of

    a. Real

    b. Imitation

    c. Apparition

    d. Dream

22. VILLAIN is the opposite of

    a. Actor

    b. Actress

    c. Queen

    d. Hero

23. VANISH is the opposite of

    a. Appear

    b. Lose

    c. Reflection

    d. Empty

24. LITERAL is the opposite of

    a. Manuscript

    b. Writing

    c. Figurative

    d. Untrue

25. HARSH is the opposite of

    a. Mild

    b. Light

    c. Bulky

    d. Bothersome

26. SPLURGE is the opposite of

a. Spend

b. Count

c. Use

d. Save

27. IDLE is the opposite of

a. Occupied

b. Vacant

c. Busy

d. Interested

28. CONSOLE is the opposite of

a. Aggravate

b. Empathize

c. Sympathize

d. Soothe

29. DERANGED is the opposite of

a. Chaos

b. Dirty

c. Bleak

d. Sane

30. DISJOINTED is the opposite of

a. Connected

b. Dismayed

c. Recognized

d. Bountiful

31. VIRAGO is a

    a. A loud domineering woman

    b. A quiet woman

    c. A load domineering Man

    d. A quiet man

32. DEPRECATE is to

    a. Approve

    b. Indifference

    c. Disapprove

    d. None of the above

33. SUCCOR is to

    a. To suck on

    b. To hate

    c. To like

    d. Give help or assistance

34. SPECIOUS means

    a. Logical

    b. Illogical

    c. Emotional

    d. 2 species

35. PROSCRIBE is to

    a. Welcome

    b. Write a prescription

    c. Banish

    d. Give a diagnosis

36. PERNICIOUS means

a. Deadly

b. Infectious

c. Common

d. Rare

37. PEDESTRIAN means

a. Rare

b. Often

c. Walking or Running

d. Commonplace

38. PETULANT means

a. Patient

b. Coquettish

c. Impatient

d. Mature

39. STINT means

a. Thrifty

b. Annoyed

c. Dislike

d. Insult

40. PRECIPITATE means

a. To rain

b. To throw down

c. To throw up

d. To snow

Answer Key

1. D
This is a part to whole relationship. A petal is to a flower as fur is to a rabbit.

2. A
A present celebrates a birthday, and a reward celebrates an accomplishment.

3. C
This is a functional relationship. A shovel is used to dig, and scissors are used to snip.

4. A
This is a parts to whole relationship. The finger is part of the hand in the same way that a leg is part of a body.

5. A
This is a cause and effect relationship. If you sleep in you will be late. If you skip breakfast you will be hungry.

6. D
A sphere is the solid form of a circle just as a cube is the solid form of a square.

7. A
This is a classification relationship. An orange is a fruit and a carrot is a vegetable.

8. D
This is a characteristic relationship. Paper is light, just as lead is heavy.

9. B
This is a composition relationship. Cars are made of steel just as windows are made of glass.

10. A
This is a symbol relation. A four-leaf clover is a symbol for luck just as a cross is a symbol for Christianity.

11. B
Conspicuous means prominent.

12. C
Benevolence means kindness.

13. A
Boisterous means loud.

14. B
Fondle means caress.

15. D
Momentous means very important.

16. C
Antagonist means enemy.

17. C
Memento means reminder.

18. D
Insidious means gradual.

19. A
Itinerary means schedule.

20. B
Illustrious means noble.

21. B
Authentic is the opposite of imitation.

22. D
Villain is the opposite of hero.

23. A
Vanish is the opposite of appear.

24. C
Literal is the opposite of figurative.

25. A
Harsh is the opposite of mild.

26. D
Splurge is the opposite of save.

27. C
Idle is the opposite of busy.

28. A
Console is the opposite of aggravate.

29. D
Deranged is the opposite of sane.

30. A
Disjointed is the opposite of connected.

31. A
Virago: Given to undue belligerence or ill manner at the slightest provocation; a shrew, a termagant.

32. C
Deprecate: To belittle or express disapproval of.

33. D
Succor: Aid, assistance or relief given to one in distress; ministration.

34. B
Specious: Seemingly well-reasoned or factual, but actually fallacious or insincere; strongly held but false.

35. C
Proscribe: Denounce or condemn, banish.

36. A
Pernicious: Causing much harm in a subtle way.

37. D
Pedestrian: Ordinary, dull; everyday; unexceptional, commonplace.

38. C
Petulant: Childishly irritable, impatient.

39. A
Stint: Thrifty, to be sparing.

40. A
Precipitate means to rain.

Help with Building your Vocabulary

Vocabulary tests can be daunting when you think of the enormous number of words that might come up in the exam. As the exam date draws near, your anxiety will grow because you know that no matter how many words you memorize, chances are, you will still remember so few. Here are some tips which you can use to hurdle the big words that may come up in your exam without having to open the dictionary and memorize all the words known to humankind.

Build up and tear apart the big words. Big words, like many other things, are composed of small parts. Some words are made up of many other words. A man who lifts weights for example, is a weight lifter. Words are also made up of word parts called prefixes, suffixes and roots. Often times, we can see the relationship of different words through these parts. A person who is skilled with both hands is ambidextrous. A word with double meaning is ambiguous. A person with two conflicting emotions is ambivalent. Two words with synonymous meanings often have the same root. Bio, a root word derived from Latin is used in words like biography meaning to write about a person's life, and biology meaning the study of living organisms.

- **Words with double meanings.** Did you know that the word husband not only means a man married to a woman, but also thrift or frugality? Sometimes, words have double meanings. The dictionary meaning, or the denotation of a word is sometimes different from the way we use it or its connotation.

- **Read widely, read deeply and read daily.** The best way to expand your vocabulary is to familiarize yourself with as many words as possible through reading. By reading, you are able to remember words in a proper context and thus, remember its meaning or at the very least, its use. Reading widely would help you get acquainted with words you may never use every day. This is the best strategy without doubt. However, if you are studying for an exam next week, or even tomorrow, it isn't much help! Below you will find a range of different ways to learn new words quickly and efficiently.

Remember! Always remember that big words are easy to understand when divided into smaller parts, and the smaller words will often have several other meanings aside from the one you already know. Below is an extensive list of root or stem words, followed by one hundred questions to help you learn word stems.

Here are suggested effective ways to help you improve your vocabulary.

- **Be Committed To Learning New Words**. To improve your vocabulary you need to make a commitment to learn new words. Commit to learning at least a word or two a day. You can also get new words by reading books, poems, stories, plays and magazines. Expose yourself to more language to increase the number of new words that you learn.

- **Learn Practical Vocabulary**. As much as possible, learn vocabulary that is associated with what you do and that you can use regularly. For example learn words related to your profession or hobby. Learn as much vocabulary as you can in your favorite subjects.

- **Use New Words Frequently**. When you learn a new word start using it and do so frequently. Repeat it when you are alone and try to use the word as often as you can with people you talk to. You can also use flashcards to practice new words that you learn.

- **Learn the Proper Usage.** If you do not understand the proper usage, look it up and make sure you have it right.

- **Use a Dictionary**. When reading textbooks, novels or assigned readings, keep the dictionary nearby. Also learn how to use online dictionaries and WORD dictionary. As soon as you come across a new word, check its meaning. If you cannot do so immediately, then you should write it down and check it when possible. This will help you understand what the word means and exactly how best to use it.

• **Learn Word Roots, Prefixes and Suffixes.** English words are usually derived from suffixes, prefixes and roots, which come from Latin, French or Greek. Learning the root or origin of a word helps you easily understand the meaning of the word and other words that are derived from the root. Generally, if you learn the meaning of one root word, you will understand two or three words. See our List of Stem Words below. This is a great two-for-one strategy. Most prefixes, suffixes, roots and stems are used in two, three or more words, so if you know the root, prefix or suffix, you can guess the meaning of many words.

• **Synonyms and Antonyms**. Most words in the English language have two or three (at least) synonyms and antonyms. For example, "big," in the most common usage, has seventy-five synonyms and an equal number of antonyms. Understanding the relationships between these words and how they all fit together gives your brain a framework, which makes them easier to learn, remember and recall.

• **Use Flash Cards**. Flash cards are the best way to memorize things. They can be used anywhere and anytime, so you can use odd free moments waiting for the bus or waiting in line. Make your own or buy commercially prepared flash cards, and keep them with you all the time.

• **Make word lists.** Learning vocabulary, like learning many things, requires repetition. Keep a new words journal in a separate section or separate notebook. Add any words that you look up in the dictionary, as well as from word lists. Review your word lists regularly.

Photocopying or printing off word lists from the Internet or handouts is not the same. Actually writing out the word and a few notes on the definition is an important process for imprinting the word in your brain. Writing out the word and definition in your New Word Journal, forces you to concentrate and focus on the new word. Hitting PRINT or pushing the button on the photocopier does not do the same thing.

How to Answer Verbal Analogies

Verbal analogies can be tricky for anyone, which is why it is important to have strategies to improve your chances of answering correctly. Here are some verbal analogies strategies that will help you answer this type question.

1. The only way to become better at anything is to practice and the same is true for verbal analogies. There really is not any other way to study for verbal analogies than by practicing them. Start a month in advance and practice an hour a day.

2. It does not matter how many relationships you can find between the words given in a verbal analogy, what is important is that you give the answer the test-maker is looking for. In other words, give the exact answer. Many times, the relationships you think you see are much more in depth than what the test maker is looking for. The following is an example of what this means:

Bigotry/Hatred

    a. sweetness: bitterness

    b. segregation: integration

    c. equality: government

    d. fanaticism: intolerance

You might automatically think that 'bigot' is to 'hate' or that 'bigots hate' is very similar to 'c.' as equality is normally associated with the government or 'd.' ad fanatics are often seen as intolerable. The problem is this way of thinking is subjective or prejudiced and not everyone thinks like this, so how can those choices be true. You will notice though, that options B and D are not a subjective thought, but a social extreme, just as 'Bigotry/hatred' is. The way to narrow down the choices is by looking at the words in as they relate to each other, 'bigotry and hatred' are similar terms, but option B is not, they are opposites. 'd.' would be the correct choice because they are also similar terms.

3. Another strategy you can use with verbal analogies is to pick out a word or words that are similar to those in the analogy. Find a word that will name the relationship of the given words. The main relationships found in analogies and are listed below:

- **Purpose:** This means that 'A' is used for 'B' the same way that 'X' is used for 'Y'.
- **Cause and Effect:** This means that 'A' has an effect on 'B' the same way that 'X' has an effect on 'Y'.
- **Part to Whole (individual to group):** This means that 'A' is a part of 'B' the same way that 'X' is a part of 'Y'
- **Part to part:** 'A' and 'B' are both parts of something the way that 'X' and 'Y' are both parts of something
- **Action to object:** 'A' is done to 'B' the same way 'X' is done to 'Y'.
- **Object to action:** 'A' does something to 'B' just as 'X' does something to 'Y'.
- **Word meaning:** 'A' means about the same as 'B' and 'X' means about the same as 'Y'
- **Opposite word meaning:** 'A means about the opposite of 'B' and 'X' means about the opposite of 'Y'
- **Sequence:** 'A' comes before (or after) B" just as 'X' comes before (or after) 'Y'.
- **Place:** 'A' and 'B' are related places just as 'X' and 'Y' are related places.
- **Magnitude:** 'A' is greater than (or less than) 'B' and 'X' is greater than (or less than) 'Y'.
- **Grammatical:** 'A' and 'B' are parts of speech related to each other-noun to noun, adjective to noun, etc.-in the same way that parts of speech 'X' and 'Y' are related to each other.

4. Read verbal analogies in sentences. If you take the example above, you could read it something like this 'Bigotry relates to hatred in the same way that'|' and insert each of the choices at the end like 'equality relates to government', etc'. You can change how you word the sentence to whichever relationship is between the words.

5. Sometimes it is difficult to identify the relationship by just looking at the analogy in the order it is represented, so switch the words and look for the relationship. Therefore, instead of considering how 'bigotry' relates to 'hatred' try to see how 'hatred' relates to 'bigotry'. If you are still stuck you can start finding relationships between the first and second word of the given analogy and the first and second word in the choices, respectively. Compare all the first words to the original first word, and the second with the second word.

6. As with all types of tests, make an educated guess when all other strategies have failed. Follow your hunches, choose a letter that you have not chosen in a while, or maybe just mark the most complex relationship you see in the choices, if you are pressed for time.

Problem Solving (PS)

THIS SECTION CONTAINS A SELF-ASSESSMENT AND PROBLEM SOLVING TUTORIAL. The tutorials are designed to familiarize general principles and the self-assessment contains general questions similar to the problem solving questions likely to be on the CFAT exam, but are not intended to be identical to the exam questions. If you do not understand parts of the tutorial, or find the tutorial difficult, it is recommended that you seek out additional instruction.

Tour of the Problem Solving Content

First, lets look at what types of questions are in the problem solving section. The CFAT has three different types of problem solving questions, word problems, sequences and visual acuity problems.

Here are examples of the three types of questions.

1. Word Problem example:

The total expense of building a fence around a square shaped field is $2000 at a rate of $5 per meter. What is the length of one side?

    a. 80 meters

    b. 100 meters

    c. 40 meters

    d. 320 meters

Answer: B

Total length of the fence will be = 2000/5 = 400 meters. This will equal to the perimeter of the square field so the length of one side will be = 400/4 = 100 meters.

2. Sequences example:

**Consider the following sequence: 6, 12, 24, 48, ...
What number should come next?**

      a. 48
      b. 64
      c. 60
      d. 96

Answer: D
The numbers doubles each time.

3. Visual Acuity Example

Select the figure with the same relationship.

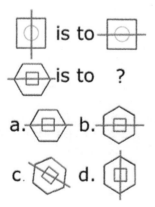

Answer: D

The relationship is the same figure flipped vertically, so the best choice is D.

Problem Solving Self-Assessment

Below is a Problem Solving self-assessment. The purpose of the self-assessment is:

- Identify your strengths and weaknesses.

- Get accustomed to the CFAT format

- Extra practice – the self-assessments are almost a full 3rd practice test!

Since this is a Self-assessment, and depending on how confident you are with problem solving questions, timing is optional. The CFAT has 30 problem solving questions to be completed in 30 minutes. The self-assessment has 25 questions, so allow about 25 minutes to complete this assessment.

The self-assessment is designed to give you a baseline score in the different areas covered. Here is a brief outline of how your score on the self-assessment relates to your understanding of the material.

75% - 100%	Excellent – you have mastered the content.
50 – 75%	Good. You have a working knowledge. Even though you can just pass this section, you may want to review the tutorials and do some extra practice to see if you can improve your mark.
25% - 50%	Below Average. You do not understand the problems. Review the tutorials, and retake this quiz again in a few days, before proceeding to the rest of the study guide.

Less than 25%	Poor. You have a very limited under-standing of the problems. Please review the tutorials, and retake this quiz again in a few days, before proceeding to the rest of the study guide.

Problem Solving Self-Assessment Answer Sheet

```
     A B C D E        A B C D E
 1  ○○○○○    21  ○○○○○
 2  ○○○○○    22  ○○○○○
 3  ○○○○○    23  ○○○○○
 4  ○○○○○    24  ○○○○○
 5  ○○○○○    25  ○○○○○
 6  ○○○○○
 7  ○○○○○
 8  ○○○○○
 9  ○○○○○
10  ○○○○○
11  ○○○○○
12  ○○○○○
13  ○○○○○
14  ○○○○○
15  ○○○○○
16  ○○○○○
17  ○○○○○
18  ○○○○○
19  ○○○○○
20  ○○○○○
```

1. Two trains leave from a station at the same time in the same direction. One with an average speed of 72 km/hr. and the other at 52 km/hr. After 20 minutes how far apart are they?

    a. 6.67 km.

    b. 17.33 km.

    c. 24.3 km.

    d. 41.33 km.

2. The average weight of 13 students in a class of 15 (two were absent that day) was 42 kg. When the remaining 2 are weighed the average became 42.7 kg. If one of the remaining students weighs 48 kg., how much does the other weigh?

    a. 44.7 kg.

    b. 45.6 kg.

    c. 47.4 kg.

    d. 46.5 kg.

3. There are some oranges in a basket. By adding 8/5 of the total to the basket the new total became 130. How many oranges were in the basket?

    a. 50

    b. 60

    c. 40

    d. 35

4. A pet store sold $19,304.56 worth of merchandise in June. If the cost of products sold was $5,284.34, employees were paid $8,384.76, and rent was $2,920.00, how much profit did the store make in June?

    a. $5,635.46

    b. $2,715.46

    c. $14,020.22

    d. $10,019.80

5. A person earns $25,000 per month and pays $9,000 income tax per year. The Government increased income tax by 0.5% per month, and his monthly earning was increased $11,000. How much more income tax does he pay per month?

    a. $750

    b. $1,050

    c. $510

    d. $1,260

6. A company gives a 12% discount to his customers on retail price. If the total is over $10,000 after the discount, they give an additional 3% discount on the remaining balance. A customer's total came to $13,500 (discounted price). How much did he save?

    a. $1,725

    b. $2,073

    c. $2,225

    d. $2,315

7. A mother is 7 times older than her child. In 25 years, her age will be double that of her child. How old is the mother now?

    a. 35

    b. 33

    c. 30

    d. 25

8. John purchased a jacket at a 7% discount. He had a membership which gave him an additional 2% discount on the discounted price. If he paid $425, what was the retail price of the jacket?

    a. $460

    b. $462

    c. $466

    d. $472

9. A square-shaped lawn has an area of 62,500 square meters. What is the cost of building a fence around it at a rate of $5.5 per meter?

    a. $4,000

    b. $5,500

    c. $4,500

    d. $5,000

10. Mr. Brown bought 5 cheese burgers, 3 drinks and 4 orders of fries for his family and a cookie pack for his dog. If the price of all single items is same at $1.30, and a 3.5% tax is added, what is the total cost of dinner?

    a. $17.00

    b. $16.90

    c. $17.50

    d. $16.00

11. Consider the following sequence: 39, 28, 19, 12, 7, ... What number should come next?

    a. 1

    b. 4

    c. 0

    d. 2

12. Consider the following sequence: 2, 3, 5, 8, ... What number should come next?

    a. 13

    b. 10

    c. 9

    d. 15

13. Consider the following sequence: 90, 85, ..., 75, 70. What is the missing number?

    a. 70

    b. 82

    c. 80

    d. 78

14. Consider the following sequence: L, O, R, ..., X
What is the missing letter?

    a. S

    b. U

    c. T

    d. M

15. Consider the following sequence: 63, 57, 52, 48, ... What number comes next?

    a. 42

    b. 37

    c. 45

    d. 40

16. Consider the sequence in row A compared to row B. What is the missing number?

A	5	20	100	3	24
B	20	80	400	12	?

    a. 96

    b. 48

    c. 64

    d. 66

17. Consider the following sequence: L, N, P, R, ? ...
What letter should come next?

    a. S

    b. T

    c. U

    d. V

18. Consider the following sequence: 3, 13, 22, 30, 37, ... What number comes next?

    a. 45

    b. 47

    c. 43

    d. 42

19. Consider the following sequence:

  ???

a.   b.   c. (star)

20. Consider the following sequence:

+ * + * | * + * + | * * + * | + + _ _

    a. + *

    b. * *

    c. + +

    d. * +

21.

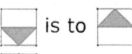 is to

 is to   ?

a. b.

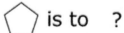

c. d.

22.

□ is to ⌐¬

⬠ is to   ?

a. ⌢   b. ⌐＼

c. ⋀   d. ⊔

23.

is to

is to   ?

a.   b.

c.   d.

24.

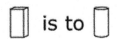 is to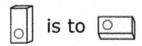

is to ?

a. ● b. ▱

c. ⬡ d. ▢

25.

is to

is to ?

a. ◯ b. ◻

c. ◉ d. ▷

Answer Key

1. A
Distance traveled by 1st train in 20 minutes = (72 × 20 minutes)/60 minutes = 24 km. Distance traveled by 2nd train in 20 minutes = (52 × 20 minutes)/60 minutes = 17.33 km. Difference in distance = 24 - 17.33 = 6.67 km.

2. D
Total weight of 13 students with average 42 will be = 42•13 = 546 kg.

The total weight of the remaining 2 will be found by subtracting the total weight of 13 students from the total weight of 15 students: 640.5 - 546 = 94.5 kg.

94.5 = the total weight of two students. One of these students weigh 48 kg, so;

The weight of the other will be = 94.5 – 48 = 46.5 kg

3. A
Suppose oranges in the basket before = x
Then: X + 8x/5 = 130
5x + 8x = 650 (Multiply both sides by 5)
13x = 650
x = 650/13
So X = 50

4. B
Total expenses = 5284.34 + 8,384.76 + 2,920.00 = 16589.10
Profit = revenue less expenses
$19,304.56 - 16589.10 = $2715.46

5. C
The income tax per year is $9,000. So, the income tax per month is 9,000/12 = $750.

This person earns $25,000 per month and pays $750 income tax. We need to find the rate of the income tax:

Tax rate: 750 * 100/25,000 = 3%

Government increased this rate by 0.5% so it became 3.5%.

The income of the person per month is increased $11,000 so it became: $25,000 + $11,000 = $36,000.

The new monthly income tax is: 36,000 * 3.5/100 = $1260.

Amount of increase in tax per month is: $1260 - $750 = $510.

6. D
To calculate the total before the 3% was taken solve the equation: 13500 = 0.97x, x = 13917.53 Then use this number to solve what the total was before the 12% discount, with the equation: 13917.53 = 0.88x. So x = 15,815.37. Then subtract 13500 from this to get a savings of $2,315

7. A
The easiest way to solve age problems is to use a table:

	Mother	Child
Now	7x	x
25 years later	7x + 25	x + 25

Now, mother is 7 times older than her child. So, if we say that the child is x years old, mother is 7x years old. In 25 years, 25 will be added to their ages. We are told that in 25 years, mother's age will double her child's age. So,

7x + 25 = 2(x + 25) ... by solving this equation, we reach x that is the child's age:

7x + 25 = 2x + 50

7x - 2x = 50 - 25

5x = 25

x = 5

Mother is 7x years old: 7x = 7 * 5 = 35

8. C
Let the original price be 100x.

At the rate of 7% discount, the discount will be
100x * 7/100 = 7x. So, the discounted price will be = 100x
- 7x = 93x.

Over this price, at the rate of 2% additional discount, the
discount will be 93x * 2/100 = 1.86x. So, the additionally
discounted price will be = 93x - 1.86x = 91.14x.

This is the amount which John has paid for the jacket:

91.14x = 425

x = 425 / 91.14 = 4.6631

The jacket costs 100x. So, 100x = 100•4.6631 = $466.31.

When rounded to the nearest whole number, this is equal
to $466.

9. B
As the lawn is square, the length of one side will be =
√62,500 = 250 meters. So the perimeter will be 250 × 4 =
1000 meters. The total cost will be 1000 × 5.5 = $5,500.

10. C
The price of all the single items is same and there are 13
total items. So the total cost will be 13 X 1.3 = $16.90. Af-
ter the 3.5% tax the total will be 16.9 X 1.035 = 17.4915,
or $17.50.

11. B
First two terms decreased by 11 and the subsequent
terms decreased by subtracting 2 from the last rate of decrease. Answer is 7 – (5 - 2) = 7 - 3 = 4.

39, [-11] 28, [-9] 19, [-7] 12, [-5] 7, [-4] 4

12. A
Each number is the sum of the previous two numbers

13. C
The numbers decrease by 5 each time.

14. B
There are two letters missing between each one, so U is next.

L, [M, N] O, [P, Q] R, [S, T] **U**, [V, W] X

15. C
The second term decreased by 6 and the next terms decreased by subtracting 5, and then 4. The answer is 48 – 3 = 45.

63 [-6] 57 [-5] 52 [-4] 48 [-3] 45

16. A
The number in row B is 4 times the number in row A.

17. B
One letter is missing after each letter. L, [M] N, [O] P, [Q] R, [S] T

18. C
The difference between the first two terms is 10. The difference between subsequent terms decreases by 1, i.e. 10, 9,8,7,6. Answer is 37 + 6 = 43.

3, [+10] 13, [+9] 22, [+8] 30, [+7] 37, [+6] 43

19. B
The sequence shifts to the left each time, so the next figure will be the square.

20. D
Each time the * and + alternate, either singly or doubles.

21. D
The relationship is the same figure flipped vertically, so the best choice is D.

22. C
The relation is the same figure with the bottom half removed.

23. D
The first pair is a rectangle with a circle inside and then an oval with a square inside. The given figures in the second pair has a triangle inside, so the match will be the circle with a square inside.

24. B
The relation is two up-right figures in the first set, and 2 horizontal figures in the second set. Choice B is the only horizontal figure.

25. C
The first pair contains a box with a circle inside, and the same figure on its side.

How to Solve Arithmetic Reasoning Problems

Most students find math word problems difficult. Tackling word problems is much easier if you have a systematic approach which we outline below.

Here is the biggest tip for studying word problems.

Practice regularly and systematically. Sounds simple and easy right? Yes it is, and yes it really does work.

Word problems are a way of thinking and require you to translate a real word problem into mathematical terms.

Some math instructors go so far as to say that learning how to think mathematically is the main reason for teaching word problems.

So what do we mean by practice regularly and systematically? Studying word problems and math in general requires a logical and mathematical frame of mind. The only way you can get this is by practicing regularly, which means everyday.

It is critical that you practice word problems everyday for the 5 days before the exam as a bare minimum.

If you practice and miss a day, you have lost the mathematical frame of mind and the benefit of your previous practice is pretty much gone. Anyone who has done any amount of math will agree – you have to practice everyday.

Everything is important. The other critical point about word problems is that all of the information given in the problem has some purpose. There is no unnecessary information! Word problems are typically around 50 words in 1 to 3 sentences. If the sometimes complicated relationships are to be explained in that short an explanation, every word has to count. Make sure that you use every piece of information.

Here are 9 simple steps to help you resolve word problems.

Step 1 – Read through the problem at least three times. The first reading should be a quick scan, and the next two reading should be done slowly with a view to finding answers to these important questions:

What does the problem ask? (Usually located towards the end of the problem)

What does the problem imply? (This is usually a point you were asked to remember).

Mark all information, and underline all important words or phrases.

Step 2 – Try to make a pictorial representation of the problem such as a circle and an arrow to indicate travel. This makes the problem a bit more real and sensible to you.

A favorite word problem is something like, 1 train leaves

Station A travelling at 100 km/hr and another train leaves Station B travelling at 60 km/hr. ...

Draw a line, the two stations, and the two trains at either end. This will help solidify the situation in your mind.

Step 3 – Use the information you have to make a table with a blank portion to indicate information you do not know.

Step 4 – Assign a single letter to represent each unknown data in your table. You can write down the unknown that each letter represents so that you do not make the error of assigning answers to the wrong unknown, because a word problem may have multiple unknowns and you will need to create equations for each unknown.

Step 5 – Translate the English terms in the word problem into a mathematical algebraic equation. Remember that the main problem is the questions is not expressed in regular math equations. Your ability to correctly identify the variables, and translate the information into an equation determines your ability to solve the problem.

Step 6 – Check the equation to see if it looks like a regular equation that you are used to seeing, and whether it looks sensible. Does the equation appear to represent the information in the question? Take note that you may need to rewrite some formulas needed to solve the word problem equation. For example, distance problems may require rewriting the distance formula, which is Distance = Time x Rate. If the word problem requires that you solve for time, instead of distance, you will need to use Distance/Rate and Distance/Time to solve for Rate. If you understand the distance word problem you should be able to identify the variable you need to solve for.

Step 7 – Use algebra rules to solve the derived equation. Take note that the laws of equation demand that what is done on this side of the equation has to also be done on the other side. You have to solve the equation so that the unknown ends up alone on one side. Where there are multiple unknowns you will need to use elimination or substitution methods to resolve all the equations.

Step 8 – Check your final answers to see if they make sense with the information given in the problem. For example if the word problem involves a discount, the final price should be less or if a product was taxed then the final answer has to cost more.

Step 9 – Cross check your answers by placing the answer or answers in the first equation to replace the unknown or unknowns. If your answer is correct then both side of the equation must equate or equal. If your answer is not correct then you may have derived a wrong equation or solved the equation wrongly. Repeat the necessary steps to correct.

Types of Arithmetic Reasoning Problems

Arithmetic Reasoning problems can be classified into 12 types. Below are examples of each type with a complete solution. Some types of word problems can be solved quickly using multiple choice strategies and some can not. Always look for ways to estimate the answer and then eliminate choices.

1. Age

A girl is 10 years older than her brother. By next year, she will be twice the age of her brother. What are their ages now?

    a. 25, 15

    b. 19, 9

    c. 21, 11

    d. 29, 19

Solution: B
We will assume that the girl's age is "a" and her brother's is "b." This means that based on the information in the

first sentence,
a = 10 + b

Next year, she will be twice her brother's age, which gives
a + 1 = 2(b+1)

We need to solve for one unknown factor and then use the answer to solve for the other. To do this we substitute the value of "a" from the first equation into the second equation. This gives

10+b + 1 = 2b + 2
11 + b = 2b + 2
11 – 2 = 2b – b
b= 9
9 = b this means that her brother is 9 years old.
Solving for the girl's age in the first equation gives

a = 10 + 9
a = 19 the girl is aged 19. So, the girl is aged 19 and the boy is 9

2. Distance or speed

Two boats travel down a river towards the same destination, starting at the same time. One of the boats is traveling at 52 km/hr, and the other boat at 43 km/hr. How far apart will they be after 40 minutes?

    a. 46.67 km

    b. 19.23 km

    c. 6.4 km

    d. 14.39 km

Solution: C

After 40 minutes, the first boat will have traveled = 52 km/hr x 40 minutes/60 minutes = 34.7 km
After 40 minutes, the second boat will have traveled = 43 km/hr x 40/60 minutes = 28.66 km
Difference between the two boats will be 34.7 km – 28.66 km = 6.04 km.

Multiple Choice Strategy

First estimate the answer. The first boat is travelling 9 km. faster than the second, for 40 minutes, which is 2/3 of an hour. 2/3 of 9 = 6, as a rough guess of the distance apart.

Choices A, B and D can be eliminated right away.

3. Ratio

The instructions in a cookbook states that 700 grams of flour must be mixed in 100 ml of water, and 0.90 grams of salt added. A cook however has just 325 grams of flour. What is the quantity of water and salt that he should use?

    a. 0.41 grams and 46.4 ml

    b. 0.45 grams and 49.3 ml

    c. 0.39 grams and 39.8 ml

    d. 0.25 grams and 40.1 ml

Solution: A

The Cookbook states 700 grams of flour, but the cook only has 325. The first step is to determine the percentage of flour he has $325/700 \times 100 = 46.4\%$
That means that 46.4% of all other items must also be used.
46.4% of 100 = 46.4 ml of water
46.4% of 0.90 = 0.41 grams of salt.

Multiple Choice Strategy

The recipe calls for 700 grams of flour but the cook only has 325, which is just less than half, the amount of water and salt are going to be approximately half.

Choices C and D can be eliminated right away. Choice B is very close so be careful. Looking closely at choice B, it is exactly half, and since 325 is slightly less than half of 700, it can't be correct.

4. Percent

An agent received $6,685 as his commission for selling a property. If his commission was 13% of the selling price, how much was the property?

  a. $68,825
  b. $121,850
  c. $49,025
  d. $51,423

Solution: D

Let's assume that the property price is x
That means from the information given, 13% of x = 6,685
Solve for x,
x = 6685 x 100/13 = $51,423

Multiple Choice Strategy

The commission, 13%, is just over 10%, which is easier to work with. Round up $6685 to $6700, and multiple by 10 for an approximate answer. 10 X 6700 = $67,000. You can do this in your head. Choice B is much too big and can be eliminated. Choice C is too small and can be eliminated. Choices A and D are left and good possibilities.

Do the calculations to make the final choice.

5. Sales & Profit

A store owner buys merchandise for $21,045. He transports them for $3,905 and pays his staff $1,450 to stock the merchandise on his shelves. If he does not incur further costs, how much does he need to sell the items to make $5,000 profit?

  a. $32,500
  b. $29,350
  c. $32,400
  d. $31,400

Solution: D

Total cost of the items is $21,045 + $3,905 + $1,450 = $26,400
Total cost is now $26,400 + $5000 profit = $31,400

Multiple Choice Strategy

Round off and add the numbers up in your head quickly. 21,000 + 4,000 + 1500 = 26500. Add in 5000 profit for a total of 31500.

Choice B is too small and can be eliminated. Choices C and A are too large and can be eliminated.

6. Tax/Income

A woman earns $42,000 per month and pays 5% tax on her monthly income. If the Government increases her monthly taxes by $1,500, what is her income after tax?

    a. $38,400
    b. $36,050
    c. $40,500
    d. $39, 500

Solution: A

Initial tax on income was $5/100 \times 42,000 = \$2,100$
$1,500 was added to the tax to give $2,100 + 1,500 = $3,600

Income after tax left is $42,000 - $3,600 = $38,400

7. Interest

A man invests $3000 in a 2-year term deposit that pays 3% interest per year. How much will he have at the end of the 2-year term?

    a. $5,200
    b. $3,020
    c. $3,182.7
    d. $3,000

Solution: C

This is a compound interest problem. The funds are invested for 2 years and interest is paid yearly, so in the second year, he will earn interest on the interest paid in the first year.

3% interest in the first year = 3/100 x 3,000 = $90
At end of first year, total amount = 3,000 + 90 = $3,090
Second year = 3/100 x 3,090 = 92.7.
At end of second year, total amount = $3090 + $92.7 = $3,182.7

8. Averaging

The average weight of 10 books is 54 grams. 2 more books were added and the average weight became 55.4. If one of the 2 new books added weighed 62.8 g, what is the weight of the other?

    a. 44.7 g
    b. 67.4 g
    c. 62 g
    d. 52 g

Solution: C

Total weight of 10 books with average 54 grams will be=10×54=540 g
Total weight of 12 books with average 55.4 will be=55.4×12=664.8 g

So total weight of the remaining 2 will be= 664.8 – 540 = 124.8 g

If one weighs 62.8, the weight of the other will be= 124.8 g – 62.8 g = 62 g

Multiple Choice Strategy

Averaging problems can be estimated by looking at which direction the average goes. If additional items are added and the average goes up, the new items much be greater than the average. If the average goes down after new items are added, the new items must be less than the average.

Here, the average is 54 grams and 2 books are added which increases the average to 55.4, so the new books must weight more than 54 grams.

Choices A and D can be eliminated right away.

9. Probability

A bag contains 15 marbles of various colors. If 3 marbles are white, 5 are red and the rest are black, what is the probability of randomly picking out a black marble from the bag?

     a. 7/15
     b. 3/15
     c. 1/5
     d. 4/15

Solution: A

Total marbles = 15
Number of black marbles = 15 – (3 + 5) = 7
Probability of picking out a black marble = 7/15

10. Two Variables

A company paid a total of $2850 to book for 6 single rooms and 4 double rooms in a hotel for one night. Another company paid $3185 to book for 13 single rooms for one night in the same hotel. What is the cost for single and double rooms in that hotel?

    a. single= $250 and double = $345

    b. single= $254 and double = $350

    c. single = $245 and double = $305

    d. single = $245 and double = $345

Solution: D

We can determine the price of single rooms from the information given of the second company. 13 single rooms = 3185.
One single room = 3185 / 13 = 245
The first company paid for 6 single rooms at $245. 245 x 6 = $1470
Total amount paid for 4 double rooms by first company = $2850 - $1470 = $1380
Cost per double room = 1380 / 4 = $345

11. Geometry

The length of a rectangle is 5 in. more than its width. The perimeter of the rectangle is 26 in. What is the width and length of the rectangle?

    a. width = 6 inches, Length = 9 inches

    b. width = 4 inches, Length = 9 inches

    c. width =4 inches, Length = 5 inches

    d. width = 6 inches, Length = 11 inches

Solution: B

Formula for perimeter of a rectangle is 2(L + W)
p=26, so 2(L+W) = p
The length is 5 inches more than the width, so
2(w+5) + 2w = 26
2w + 10 + 2w = 26
2w + 2w = 26 - 10
4w = 16

W = 16/4 = 4 inches

L is 5 inches more than w, so L = 5 + 4 = 9 inches.

12. Totals and fractions

A basket contains 125 oranges, mangos and apples. If 3/5 of the fruits in the basket are mangos and only 2/5 of the mangos are ripe, how many ripe mangos are there in the basket?

   a. 30
   b. 68
   c. 55
   d. 47

Solution: A
Number of mangos in the basket is 3/5 x 125 = 75
Number of ripe mangos = 2/5 x 75 = 30

Sequences Tutorial

Answering sequence questions is a skill of recognizing patterns, and the best way to improve is to familiarize yourself with the different types, and to practice. Here is a typical example:

Consider the following series: 26, 21, ..., 11, 6. What is the missing number?
   a. 27
   b. 23
   c. 16
   d. 29

Looking carefully at the sequence, we can see right away that each number is 5 less than the previous number, so the missing number is 16.

We can re-write this sequence in mathematical notation as, a^1, a^2, a^3, ... a^n, where n is an integer and a^n is called its nth term. And we can write the sequence as a formula, where an integer is substituted in the place of the variable in the formula and the terms are obtained.

For example, let us consider the sequence 5,10,15,20,...

- Here, $a^n = 5^n$. The formula $a^n = 5^n$.

- The nth term of a sequence can be found by plugging n into the formula for the sequence. So for example, if we wanted to find the 100th number in this sequence, we would substitute n=100 in the formula and get 500.

Types of Number Sequence Problems

1. Simple addition or subtraction – each number in the sequence is obtained by adding a number to the previous number.

For example,   2, 5, 8, 11, 14

Note: the notation used here denotes the number in the sequence, so, $a^1 = 1$ and $a^2 = 5$. The superscript numbers are NOT exponents.

Each number in the sequence is obtained by adding 3 to the previous number, which we could write as, $a^{n+1} = a^n + 3$. Or, simpler still, if n = 1, then $a^1 = 2$ from the given information, and a^2 is 5. So, $a^{n+1} = a^n + 3$, or $a^2 = a^1 + 3$.

2. Simple multiplication - each number in the sequence is obtained by multiplying the previous number by a whole number or fraction.

For example,   3, 6, 18, 54

Or,

20, 10, 5, 2.5

Each number in the first sequence is obtained by multiplying the previous number by 3, which we could write as, $a^{n+1} = a^n \times 3$.

In the second example, each number in the series is the previous number divided by 2, or multiplied by ½, or $a^{n+1} = a^n \times ½$.

3. Prime Numbers – each number in the sequence is a prime number.

For example,

23, ... , 31, 37

Answer: 29

4. Operations on the previous two numbers

For example,

8, 14, 22, 36, 58

Here the sequence is created by adding the previous 2 numbers.

5. Exponents

The number sequence is created by each number squared or cubed.

For example,

3, 9, 81, 6561, where each number is squared.

6. Combining Sequences

2, 7, 13, 20, 28, 37

Here the sequence starts with 2, and each element is added to another sequence starting with 5. So, 2 + 5 = 7, 7 + 6 = 13, 13 + 7 = 20 and so on.

A variation is a sequence with a repeating element. For example,

1, 2, 3, 5, 7, 9, 12, 15

Here the sequence is, for each n, +1, +1, +1, +2, +2, +2, +3, +3,

7. Fractions

For example,

16/4, 4/2, 2/2, 1/2

Fractions are often meant to confuse. If fractions don't have an obvious relationship, reduce them to lowest terms or to whole numbers. Reducing these to whole numbers, gives,

4, 2, 1, ½

Right away, we can see the numbers are half the previous number, so the next in the series is ¼.

In this example, the answer is a fraction; however, you may have to reduce fractions to see the relation, and then convert back to get the answer in the correct form.

Strategy for Answering Sequence Questions

Here is a quick method that will help you answer number series.

For example:

2, 5, 6, 7, 8,

Step 1 – glance at the series quickly and see if you can spot the pattern right away.

Step 2 – Start analyzing.

Take the different between the first 2 numbers and the different between the second 2 numbers.

2, (+3) 5, (+1) 6, (+1) 7, (+1) 8,

No clear pattern with a simple analysis. There is no addition, subtraction, multiplication, division, fractional or exponent relationship.

The relation must be a higher order or a second series.

Next look at the relation between the 1st number and the 2nd and the 1st and the 3rd.   We see that,

1st + 3 = 5, 1st + 4 = 6. That's it!   The number 2 is added to the sequence, 3, 4, 5, 6, so the next number will be 2 + 7 = 9.

Spatial Ability (SA)

THIS SECTION CONTAINS A SELF-ASSESSMENT AND SPATIAL ABILITY TUTORIAL. The tutorials are designed to familiarize with general principles and the self-assessment contains general questions similar to the spatial ability questions likely to be on the CFAT exam, but are not intended to be identical to the exam questions. If you do not understand parts of the tutorial, or find the tutorial difficult, it is recommended that you seek out additional instruction.

Spatial Ability Self-Assessment

The purpose of the self-assessment is:

- Identify your strengths and weaknesses.

- Get accustomed to the CFAT format

- Extra practice – the self-assessments are almost a full 3rd practice test!

Since this is a Self-assessment, and depending on how confident you are with spatial ability, timing is optional. The CFAT has 15 spatial ability questions to be completed in 15 minutes. The self-assessment has 10 questions, so allow about 10 minutes to complete this assessment.

The self-assessment is designed to give you a baseline score in the different areas covered. Here is a brief outline of how your score on the self-assessment relates to your understanding of the material.

75% - 100%	Excellent – you have mastered the content.
50 – 75%	Good. You have a working knowledge. Even though you can just pass this section, you may want to review the tutorials and do some extra practice to see if you can improve your mark.
25% - 50%	Below Average. You do not under-stand the problems. Review the tutorials, and retake this quiz again in a few days, before pro-ceeding to the rest of the study guide.
Less than 25%	Poor. You have a very limited under-standing of the problems. Please review the Tutorials, and retake this quiz again in a few days, before proceeding to the rest of the study guide.

The questions below are not the same as you will find on the CFAT - that would be too easy! And nobody knows what the questions will be and they change all the time. Below are general spatial ability questions. So, while the format and exact wording of the questions may differ slightly, and change from year to year, if you can answer the questions below, you will have no problem with the spatial ability section of the CFAT.

Spatial Ability Self-Assessment
Answer Sheet

	A	B	C	D
1	○	○	○	○
2	○	○	○	○
3	○	○	○	○
4	○	○	○	○
5	○	○	○	○
6	○	○	○	○
7	○	○	○	○
8	○	○	○	○
9	○	○	○	○
10	○	○	○	○

1. When the two longest sides touch what will the shape be?

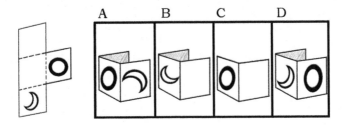

2. When folded, what pattern is possible?

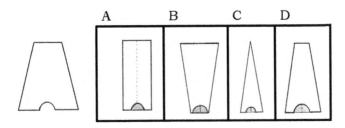

3. When folded into a loop, what will the strip of paper look like?

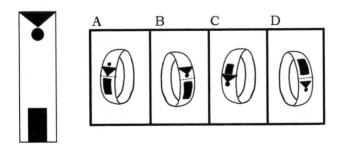

4. Which of the choices is the same pattern at a different angle?

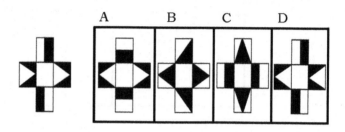

5. When put together, what 3-dimensional shape will you get?

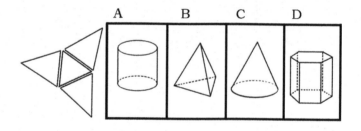

6. When folded, what pattern is possible?

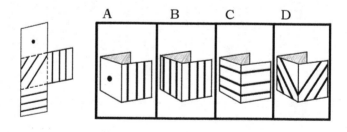

7. When folded into a loop, what will the strip of paper look like?

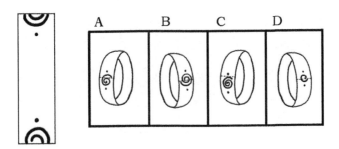

8. Which of the choices is the same pattern at a different angle?

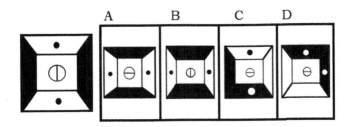

9. When folded, which shape will you get?

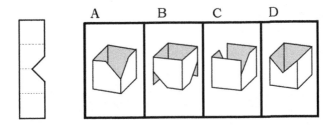

10. When folded, what pattern is possible?

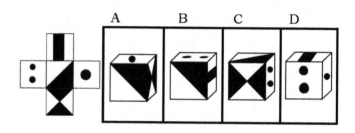

Answer Key

1. D

2. B

3. C

4. B

5. B

6. C

7. B

8. A

9. A

10. A

Practice Test Questions Set 1

THE PRACTICE TEST PORTION PRESENTS QUESTIONS THAT ARE REPRESENTATIVE OF THE TYPE OF QUESTION YOU SHOULD EXPECT TO FIND ON THE CFAT. The questions below are not the same as you will find on the CFAT - that would be too easy! And nobody knows what the questions will be and they change all the time. Below are general questions that cover the same areas as the CFAT. So, while the format and exact wording of the questions may differ slightly, and change from year to year, if you can answer the questions below, you will have no problem with the CFAT.

For the best results, take these practice test questions as if it were the real exam. Set aside time when you will not be disturbed, and a location that is quiet and free of distractions. Read the instructions carefully, read each question carefully, and answer to the best of your ability.

Use the bubble answer sheets provided. When you have completed the practice test questions, check your answer against the answer key and read the explanation provided.

Verbal Ability Answer Sheet

	A	B	C	D	E		A	B	C	D	E
1	○	○	○	○	○	21	○	○	○	○	○
2	○	○	○	○	○	22	○	○	○	○	○
3	○	○	○	○	○	23	○	○	○	○	○
4	○	○	○	○	○	24	○	○	○	○	○
5	○	○	○	○	○	25	○	○	○	○	○
6	○	○	○	○	○	26	○	○	○	○	○
7	○	○	○	○	○	27	○	○	○	○	○
8	○	○	○	○	○	28	○	○	○	○	○
9	○	○	○	○	○	29	○	○	○	○	○
10	○	○	○	○	○	30	○	○	○	○	○
11	○	○	○	○	○						
12	○	○	○	○	○						
13	○	○	○	○	○						
14	○	○	○	○	○						
15	○	○	○	○	○						
16	○	○	○	○	○						
17	○	○	○	○	○						
18	○	○	○	○	○						
19	○	○	○	○	○						
20	○	○	○	○	○						

Spatial Ability Answer Sheet

1. (A)(B)(C)(D)   11. (A)(B)(C)(D)

2. (A)(B)(C)(D)   12. (A)(B)(C)(D)

3. (A)(B)(C)(D)   13. (A)(B)(C)(D)

4. (A)(B)(C)(D)   14. (A)(B)(C)(D)

5. (A)(B)(C)(D)   15. (A)(B)(C)(D)

6. (A)(B)(C)(D)

7. (A)(B)(C)(D)

8. (A)(B)(C)(D)

9. (A)(B)(C)(D)

10. (A)(B)(C)(D)

Problem Solving Ability Answer Sheet

	A	B	C	D	E		A	B	C	D	E
1	○	○	○	○	○	21	○	○	○	○	○
2	○	○	○	○	○	22	○	○	○	○	○
3	○	○	○	○	○	23	○	○	○	○	○
4	○	○	○	○	○	24	○	○	○	○	○
5	○	○	○	○	○	25	○	○	○	○	○
6	○	○	○	○	○	26	○	○	○	○	○
7	○	○	○	○	○	27	○	○	○	○	○
8	○	○	○	○	○	28	○	○	○	○	○
9	○	○	○	○	○	29	○	○	○	○	○
10	○	○	○	○	○	30	○	○	○	○	○
11	○	○	○	○	○						
12	○	○	○	○	○						
13	○	○	○	○	○						
14	○	○	○	○	○						
15	○	○	○	○	○						
16	○	○	○	○	○						
17	○	○	○	○	○						
18	○	○	○	○	○						
19	○	○	○	○	○						
20	○	○	○	○	○						

1. SUCCULENT means the same as

 a. Dull

 b. Adventurous

 c. Sweet

 d. Juicy

2. CONSTRUE means the same as

 a. Decide

 b. Design

 c. Interpret

 d. Examine

3. INDUSTRIOUS means the same as

 a. Sad

 b. Hard working

 c. Loving

 d. Funny

4. HESITANT means the same as

 a. Willing

 b. Doubtful

 c. Eager

 d. Happy

5. LUCID means the same as

 a. Dark

 b. Clear

 c. Memorable

 d. Easy

6. PECULIAR means the same as

a. New

b. Strange

c. Imaginative

d. Funny

7. VIVID means the same as

a. Glamorous

b. Bountiful

c. Varied

d. Brilliant

8. SEMBLANCE means the same as

a. Personality

b. Appearance

c. Attitude

d. Ambition

9. CONFUSED is the opposite of

a. Frustrated

b. Ashamed

c. Enlightened

d. Unknown

10. LIAISE is the opposite of

a. Uncoordinated

b. Coordinate

c. Combine

d. Encourage

11. ILLICIT is the opposite of

    a. Unlawful

    b. Legal

    c. Anonymous

    d. Deceitful

12. STERILE is the opposite of

    a. Dirty

    b. Alcoholic

    c. Drunk

    d. Drug

13. MYRIAD is the opposite of

    a. Many

    b. Abundant

    c. Few

    d. Plenty

14. PESSIMISTIC is the opposite of

    a. Optimistic

    b. Jovial

    c. Joyful

    d. Deliberate

15. PLACID is the opposite of

    a. Chaotic

    b. Confusing

    c. Peaceful

    d. Silent

16. STURDY is the opposite of

  a. Strong

  b. Kind

  c. Rough

  d. Flimsy

17. IMPORTUNE means

  a. To find an opportunity

  b. To ask all the time.

  c. Cannot find an opportunity

  d. None of the above

18. VOLATILE means

  a. Not explosive

  b. Catches fire easily

  c. Does not catch fire

  d. Explosive

19. PLAINTIVE means

  a. Happy

  b. Mournful

  c. Faint

  d. Plain

20. NEXUS means

  a. A connection

  b. A telephone switch

  c. Part of a computer

  d. None of the above

21. INHERENT means

    a. To receive money in a will

    b. An essential part of

    c. To receive money from a will

    d. None of the above

22. TORPID means

    a. Fast

    b. Rapid

    c. Sluggish

    d. Violent

23. GREGARIOUS means

    a. Sociable

    b. Introverted

    c. Large

    d. Solitary

24. NEST is to BIRD as CAVE is to

    a. Bear

    b. Petal

    c. House

    d. Dog

25. TEACHER is to SCHOOL as WAITRESS is to

    a. Office

    b. Coffee shop

    c. Customer

    d. Student

26. PEBBLE is to BOULDER as POND is to

    a. Ocean

    b. River

    c. Drop

    d. Rapids

27. DOG is to POODLE as SHARK is to

    a. Great white

    b. Dolphin

    c. Whale

    d. Fish

28. FOX is to CHICKEN as CAT is to

    a. Rabbit

    b. Mouse

    c. Cat

    d. Hen

29. LAWYER is to TRIAL as DOCTOR is to

    a. Patient

    b. Businessman

    c. Operation

    d. Nurse

30. EAT is to FAT as BREATHE is to

    a. Inhale

    b. Live

    c. Drink

    d. Talk

Part II - Spatial Ability

1. When folded, which shape is possible?

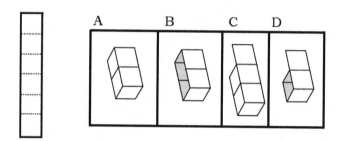

2. When folded, what pattern is possible?

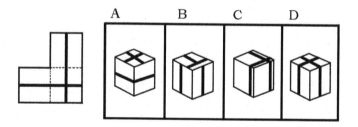

3. When folded into a loop, what will the strip of paper look like?

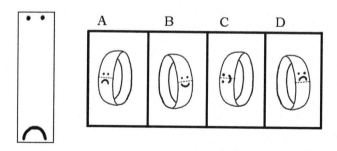

4. Which of the choices is the same pattern at a different angle?

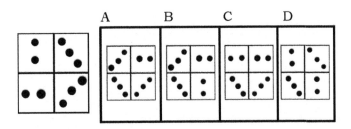

5. When folded along the dotted lines, which shape will you get?

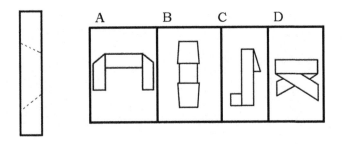

6. When folded, what pattern is possible?

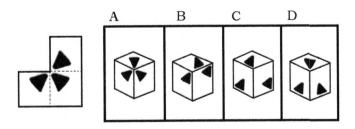

7. When folded into a loop, what will the strip of paper look like?

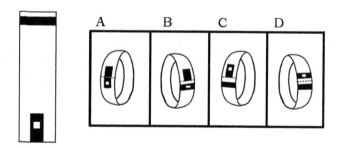

8. Which of the choices is the same pattern at a different angle?

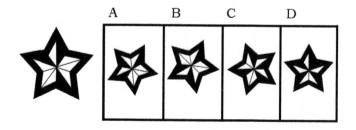

9. When folded along the dotted line, which shape will you get?

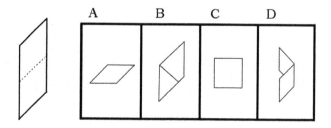

10. When folded, what pattern is possible?

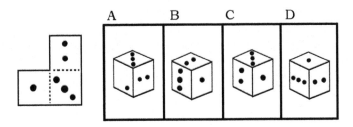

11. When folded, what pattern is possible?

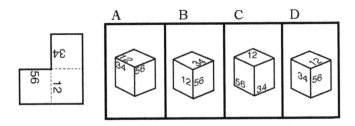

12. When folded into a loop, what will the strip of paper look like?

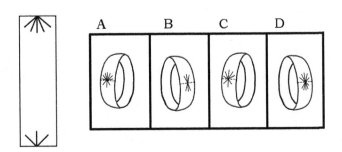

13. Which of the choices is the same pattern at a different angle?

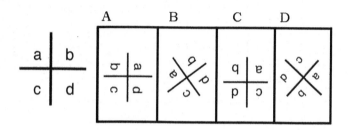

14. When folded, what pattern is possible?

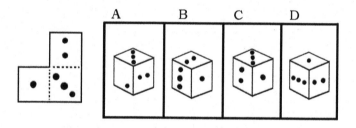

15. Which of the choices is the same pattern at a different angle?

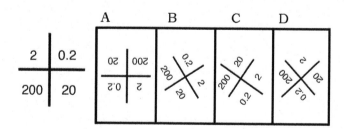

Part III - Problem Solving

**1. Consider the following sequence: 25, 33, 41, 49, ...
What number should come next?**

    a. 51

    b. 55

    c. 59

    d. 57

**2. Consider the following sequence: 6, 11, 18, 27, ...
What number should come next?**

    a. 38

    b. 35

    c. 29

    d. 30

3. Consider Box A and the relationship to the numbers in Box B. What is the missing number in Box B?

Box A

6	3
9	5

Box B

36	?
81	25

    a. 49

    b. 51

    c. 9

    d. 12

**4. Consider the following sequence: 13, 26, 52, 104, ...
What number should come next?**

     a. 208

     b. 106

     c. 200

     d. 400

**5. Consider the following sequence: 32, 26, 20, 14, ...
What number should come next?**

     a. 12

     b. 19

     c. 10

     d. 8

**6. Consider the following sequence: 12, 4, 16, ..., 36.
What is the missing number?**

     a. 18

     b. 22

     c. 20

     d. 30

**7. Consider the following sequence: 3, 9, 27, ..., 243.
What is the missing number?**

     a. 30

     b. 39

     c. 18

     d. 81

**8. Consider the following sequence: 6, 12, 24, 48, ...
What number should come next?**

    a. 48

    b. 64

    c. 60

    d. 96

**9. Consider the following sequence: 5, 6, 11, 17, ...
What number should come next?**

    a. 28

    b. 34

    c. 36

    d. 27

**10. Consider the following sequence: 26, 21, ..., 11, 6.
What is the missing number?**

    a. 27

    b. 23

    c. 16

    d. 29

11. There are 15 yellow and 35 orange balls in a basket. How many more yellow balls must be added to make the yellow balls 65%?

    a. 50

    b. 35

    c. 65

    d. 70

12. The length of a rectangle is twice its width and its area is equal to the area of a square with 12 cm. sides. What will be the perimeter of the rectangle to the nearest whole number?

    a. 51 cm.

    b. 36 cm.

    c. 46 cm.

    d. 56 cm.

13. A distributor purchased 550 kilograms of potatoes for $165. He distributed these at a rate of $6.4 per 20 kilograms to 15 shops, $3.4 per 10 kilograms to 12 shops and the remainder at $1.8 per 5 kilograms. If his total distribution cost is $10, what will his profit be?

    a. $8.60

    b. $24.60

    c. $14.90

    d. $23.40

14. 5 men have to share a load weighing 10 kg 550 g equally. How much will each man have to carry? 1 kilogram = 1000 grams.

    a. 900 g

    b. 1.5 kg

    c. 3 kg

    d. 2 kg 110 g

15. A worker's weekly salary was increased by 30%. If his new salary is $150, what was his old salary?

    a. $120

    b. $99.15

    c. $109

    d. $115.4

16. How much pay does Mr. Johnson receive if he gives half to his family, pays $250 for rent, and has exactly 3/7 of his pay left over?

    a. $3,600

    b. $2,800

    c. $1,750

    d. $3,500

17. Smith and Simon are playing a card game. Smith will win if a card drawn from a deck of 52 is either 7 or a diamond, and Simon will win if the drawn card is an even number. Which statement is more likely to be correct?

    a. Simon will win more games.

    b. Smith will win more games

    c. They have same chance of winning.

    d. A decision can not be made from the data provided.

18. Mr. White wants to tile his rectangular back yard which is 16 meters × 11 meters. The dimensions of each tile are 7 cm × 4 cm. If cost of each tile is $0.30 and 2.5% tiles break during handling. How much will it cost?

    a. $18,857

    b. $19,328

    c. $20,895

    d. $21,563

19. A map uses a scale of 1:2,000   How much distance on the ground is 5.2 inches on the map if the scale is in inches?

    a. 100,400

    b. 10, 500

    c. 10,400

    d. 10,400

20. If a train travels at 72 kilometers per hour, what distance it will cover in 12 seconds?

    a. 200 meters

    b. 220 meters

    c. 240 meters

    d. 260 meters

21. Tony bought 15 dozen eggs for \$80. 16 eggs were broken during loading and unloading. The remaining he sold at \$0.54 each. What will be his percentage profit? Provide answer in 2 significant digits.

    a. 11%

    b. 11.20%

    c. 11.50%

    d. 12%

22.

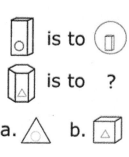

23.

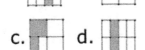

24.

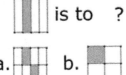

a. b.

c. d.

25.

26.

□ is to ▪

△ is to ?

a. ⬠• b. △••

c. △• d. ⬡•

27.

□ is to □ ⬠

⬠ is to ?

a. ⬠ ⬡ b. □ ⬡

c. ⬠ ○ d. ○ ⬡

28.

⊔ is to ∠⟍

⊍ is to ?

a. ⌣ b. ⊲⟍

c. ⊔ d. ∠⟍

29.

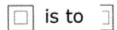

is to ⌐

⬠ is to ?

a. ⟩   b. ⟩

c. ⟩   d. ⌐

30.

☐ is to ⌐

⬠ is to ?

a.)   b. ⟩

c.)   d. ⌐

Answer Key

1. D
Succulent means the same as juicy.

2. C
Construe means the same as interpret.

3. B
Industrious means the same as hard working.

4. B
Hesitant means the same as doubtful.

5. B
Lucid means the same as clear.

6. B
Peculiar means the same as strange.

7. D
Vivid means the same as brilliant.

8. B
Semblance means the same as appearance.

9. C
Confused is the opposite of enlightened.

10. A
Liaise is the opposite of uncoordinated.

11. B
Illicit is the opposite of legal.

12. A
Sterile is the opposite of dirty.

13. C
Myriad is the opposite of few.

14. A
Pessimistic is the opposite of optimistic.

15. A
Placid is the opposite of chaotic.

16. D
Sturdy is the opposite of flimsy.

17. B
Importune: To harass with persistent requests.

18. D
Volatile: explosive; liable to change rapidly and unpredictably.

19. B
Plaintive: Sorrowful, mournful or melancholic.

20. A
Nexus: A form of connection.

21. B
Inherent: Naturally a part or consequence of something, an essential part of.

22. C
Torpid: Lazy, lethargic or apathetic.

23. A
Gregarious: Describing one who enjoys being in crowds and socializing.

24. A
This is a functional relationship. A bird lives in a nest, the same way that a bear lives in a cave.

25. B
This is a functional relationship. A teacher works in a school in the same way that a waitress works in a coffee shop.

26. A
This is a degree relationship. A boulder is a very large pebble - both are rocks, in the same way that an ocean is a very large pond - both are bodies of water.

27. A
This is a type relationship. A poodle is a type of dog in the same way that a great white is a type of shark.

28. B
This is a predator/prey relationship. Foxes eat chickens in the same way that cats eat mice.

29. C
This is a functional relationship. A lawyer defends a client in a trial in the same way that a doctor heals a patient in an operation.

30. B
This is a cause and effect relationship. You must eat to become fat, in the same way that you must breathe to live.

Spatial Ability

1. **B**

2. **D**

3. **B**

4. **D**

5. **A**

6. **A**

7. **C**

8. **B**

9. **D**

10. **C**

11. **D**

12. **A**

13. **D**

14. **C**

15. **A**

Problem Solving

1. D
The numbers increase by 8.

2. A
The interval begins with 5, and increases by 2 and is
added each time.
6, [+5] 11, [+7] 18, [+9] 27 [+11] **38**

3. C
The numbers in Box B are squares of the numbers in
Box A.

4. A
The number doubles each time.

5. D
The numbers decrease by 6 each time.

6. C
Each number is the sum of the previous two numbers.

7. D
The number triples each time.

8. D
The numbers doubles each time.

9. A
Each number is the sum of the previous two numbers

10. C
The numbers decrease by 5 each time.

11. A
There are 50 balls in the basket now. Let x be the number
of yellow balls that are to be added to make yellow balls
65%. The equation becomes $((X + 15)/X)] + 50 = 65/100$.
X = 50.

12. A
Area of the square = $12 \times 12 = 144$ cm^2. Let x be the width so
2x will be the length of rectangle. The area will be $2x^2$ and

the perimeter will be 2(2x+x) = 6x. According to the condition 2x² = 144 then x = 8.48cm. The perimeter will be 6 × 8.48 = 50.88 = 51 cm.

13. A

The distribution is done in three different rates and amounts:

$6.4 per 20 kilograms to 15 shops ... 20•15 = 300 kilograms distributed

$3.4 per 10 kilograms to 12 shops ... 10•12 = 120 kilograms distributed

550 - (300 + 120) = 550 - 420 = 130 kilograms left. This amount is distributed by 5 kilogram portions. So, this means that there are 130/5 = 26 shops.

$1.8 per 130 kilograms.

We need to find the amount he earned overall these distributions.

$6.4 per 20 kilograms : 6.4•15 = $96 for 300 kilograms

$3.4 per 10 kilograms : 3.4•12 = $40.8 for 120 kilograms

$1.8 per 5 kilograms : 1.8•26 = $46.8 for 130 kilograms

So, he earned 96 + 40.8 + 46.8 = $ 183.6

The total distribution cost is given as $10

The profit is found by: Money earned - money spent ... It is important to remember that he bought 550 kilograms of potatoes for $165 at the beginning:

Profit = 183.6 - 10 - 165 = $8.6

14. D

First, we need to convert all units to grams. Since 1000 g = 1 kg:

10 kg 550 g = 10•1000 g + 550 g = 10,000 g + 550 g = 10,550 g.

10,550 g is shared between 5 men. So each man will have to carry 10,550/5 = 2,110 g

2,110 g = 2,000 g + 110 g = 2 kg 110 g

15. D
Let old salary = X, therefore $150 = x + 0.30x, 150 = 1x + 0.30x, 150 = 1.30x, x = 150/1.30 =115.3846 = 115.38 = 115.4

16. D
We check the fractions taking place in the question. We see that there is a "half" (that is 1/2) and 3/7. So, we multiply the denominators of these fractions to decide how to name the total money. We say that Mr. Johnson has 14x at the beginning; he gives half of this, meaning 7x, to his family. $250 to his landlord. He has 3/7 of his money left. 3/7 of 14x is equal to:

14x•(3/7) = 6x

So,

Spent money is: 7x + 250

Unspent money is: 6x

Total money is: 14x

We write an equation: total money = spent money + unspent money

14x = 7x + 250 + 6x

14x - 7x - 6x = 250

x = 250

We are asked to find the total money that is 14x:

14x = 14•250 = $3500

17. A
There are 52 cards in total. Smith has 16 cards in which

he can win. So his winning probability in a single game will be 16/52. Simon has 20 cards where he will win, so his probability of a win in a single draw is 20/52. Simon has a greater chance of winning.

18. B
The area of each tile is 7 cm. X 4 cm. = 28 cm^2. The area of the yard is 16 m X 11 m = 176 m^2 = 1760000 cm^2. The number of tiles required is 1760000/28 = 62857. 2.5% of the tiles break during handling, so 1.025 X 62857 = 64429. Total cost will be 64429 X 0.3 = $19,328.

19. C
1 inch on map = 2,000 inches on ground. So, 5.2 inches on map = 5.2•2,000 = 10,400 inches on ground.

20. C
1 hour is equal to 3,600 seconds and 1 kilometer is equal to 1000 meters.

Since this train travels 72 kilometers per hour, this means that it covers 72,000 meters in 3,600 seconds.

If it travels 72,000 meters in 3,600 seconds

It travels x meters in 12 seconds

By cross multiplication: x = 72,000 • 12 / 3,600

x = 240 meters

21. A
Let us first mention the money Tony spent: $80

Now we need to find the money Tony earned:

He had 15 dozen eggs = 15•12 = 180 eggs. 16 eggs were broken. So,

Remaining number of eggs that Tony sold = 180 – 16 = 164.

Total amount he earned for selling 164 eggs = 164•0.54 = $88.56.

As a summary, he spent $80 and earned $88.56.

The profit is the difference: 88.56 - 80 = $8.56

Percent profit is found by proportioning the profit to the money he spent:

8.56•100/80 = 10.7%

Checking the answers, we round 10.7 to the nearest whole number: 11%

22. C
The inside and larger shapes are reversed.

23. D
The shaded area is divided in half in the second figure.

24. D
The relation is the same figure rotated to the right.

25. B
The relation is the number of dots in the first figure is one-half the number of sides in the second figure.

26. C
The pattern is the same figure with a dot inside.

27. C
The relation is the same figure smaller, plus another figure with one more side.

28. B
The relation is the bottom half of the 3-dimensional figure.

29. C
The relation is the right half of the first object.

30. B
The relation is the right half of the first object.

Practice Test Questions Set 2

THE PRACTICE TEST PORTION PRESENTS QUESTIONS THAT ARE REPRESENTATIVE OF THE TYPE OF QUESTION YOU SHOULD EXPECT TO FIND ON THE CFAT. The questions below are not the same as you will find on the CFAT - that would be too easy! And nobody knows what the questions will be and they change all the time. Below are general questions that cover the same areas as the CFAT. So, while the format and exact wording of the questions may differ slightly, and change from year to year, if you can answer the questions below, you will have no problem with the CFAT.

For the best results, take these practice test questions as if it were the real exam. Set aside time when you will not be disturbed, and a location that is quiet and free of distractions. Read the instructions carefully, read each question carefully, and answer to the best of your ability.

Use the bubble answer sheets provided. When you have completed the practice test questions, check your answer against the answer key and read the explanation provided.

Verbal Ability Answer Sheet

	A	B	C	D	E			A	B	C	D	E
1	○	○	○	○	○		21	○	○	○	○	○
2	○	○	○	○	○		22	○	○	○	○	○
3	○	○	○	○	○		23	○	○	○	○	○
4	○	○	○	○	○		24	○	○	○	○	○
5	○	○	○	○	○		25	○	○	○	○	○
6	○	○	○	○	○		26	○	○	○	○	○
7	○	○	○	○	○		27	○	○	○	○	○
8	○	○	○	○	○		28	○	○	○	○	○
9	○	○	○	○	○		29	○	○	○	○	○
10	○	○	○	○	○		30	○	○	○	○	○
11	○	○	○	○	○							
12	○	○	○	○	○							
13	○	○	○	○	○							
14	○	○	○	○	○							
15	○	○	○	○	○							
16	○	○	○	○	○							
17	○	○	○	○	○							
18	○	○	○	○	○							
19	○	○	○	○	○							
20	○	○	○	○	○							

Spatial Ability Answer Sheet

	A	B	C	D
1	○	○	○	○
2	○	○	○	○
3	○	○	○	○
4	○	○	○	○
5	○	○	○	○
6	○	○	○	○
7	○	○	○	○
8	○	○	○	○
9	○	○	○	○
10	○	○	○	○
11	○	○	○	○
12	○	○	○	○
13	○	○	○	○
14	○	○	○	○
15	○	○	○	○

Problem Solving Ability Answer Sheet

	A	B	C	D	E		A	B	C	D	E
1	○	○	○	○	○	21	○	○	○	○	○
2	○	○	○	○	○	22	○	○	○	○	○
3	○	○	○	○	○	23	○	○	○	○	○
4	○	○	○	○	○	24	○	○	○	○	○
5	○	○	○	○	○	25	○	○	○	○	○
6	○	○	○	○	○	26	○	○	○	○	○
7	○	○	○	○	○	27	○	○	○	○	○
8	○	○	○	○	○	28	○	○	○	○	○
9	○	○	○	○	○	29	○	○	○	○	○
10	○	○	○	○	○	30	○	○	○	○	○
11	○	○	○	○	○						
12	○	○	○	○	○						
13	○	○	○	○	○						
14	○	○	○	○	○						
15	○	○	○	○	○						
16	○	○	○	○	○						
17	○	○	○	○	○						
18	○	○	○	○	○						
19	○	○	○	○	○						
20	○	○	○	○	○						

Part I - Verbal Skills

1. JARGON means the same as

    a. Slang

    b. Slander

    c. Plagiarism

    d. Outdated

2. RENDER means the same as

    a. Give

    b. Recognize

    c. Stem

    d. Adjust

3. INTRUSIVE means the same as

    a. Private

    b. Invasive

    c. Mysterious

    d. Unique

4. RENOWN means the same as

    a. Popular

    b. Safe

    c. Shy

    d. Curtail

5. INCOHERENT means the same as

a. Ambiguous

b. Lighthearted

c. Jumbled

d. Malignant

6. CONGENIAL means the same as

a. Pleasant

b. Distort

c. Valuable

d. Liability

7. BERATE means the same as

a. Criticize

b. Unspoken

c. Tenet

d. Turf

8. SATE means the same as

a. Inadequate

b. Satisfy

c. Lacking

d. Spectator

9. ABUNDANT is the opposite of

a. Scarce

b. Plenty

c. Analysis

d. Obtrusive

10. TOUGH is the opposite of

    a. Bully

    b. Gregarious

    c. Weak

    d. Massive

11. SIMPLE is the opposite of

    a. Complex

    b. Plain

    c. Shy

    d. Vibrant

12. EXHIBIT is the opposite of

    a. Elevate

    b. Conceal

    c. Brood

    d. Contest

13. STINGY is the opposite of

    a. Tight

    b. Offensive

    c. Mean

    d. Generous

14. ADVANCE is the opposite of

    a. New

    b. Retreat

    c. Next

    d. Followed

15. CEASE is the opposite of

a. Halt

b. Amidst

c. Delay

d. Begin

16. IMMENSE is the opposite of

a. Scary

b. Honor

c. Tiny

d. Loud

17. REDUNDANT means

a. Backup

b. Necessary repetition

c. Unnecessary repetition

d. No repetition

18. BICKER means

a. Chat

b. Discuss

c. Argue

d. Debate

19. SOMBRE means

a. Gothic

b. Black

c. Gloomy

d. Evil

20. MAVERICK means

   a. Rebel

   b. Conformist

   c. Unconventional

   d. Conventional

21. TENUOUS means

   a. Strong

   b. Tense

   c. Firm

   d. Weak

22. Pandemonium means

   a. Chaos

   b. Orderly

   c. Quiet

   d. Noisy

23. Perpetual means

   a. Continuous

   b. Slowly

   c. Over a very long time

   d. Motion

24. MELT is to LIQUID as FREEZE is to

   a. Ice

   b. Condense

   c. Solid

   d. Steam

25. CLOCK is to TIME as THERMOMETER is to

    a. Heat

    b. Radiation

    c. Energy

    d. Temperature

26. CAR is to GARAGE as PLANE is to

    a. Depot

    b. Port

    c. Hanger

    d. Harbour

27. ACTING is to THEATER as GAMBLING is to

    a. Gym

    b. Bar

    c. Club

    d. Casino

28. PORK is to PIG as BEEF is to

    a. Herd

    b. Farmer

    c. Cow

    d. Lamb

29. FRUIT is to BANANA as MAMMAL is to

    a. Rabbit

    b. Snake

    c. Fish

    d. Sparrow

30. **SLUMBER is to SLEEP as BOG is to**

    a. Dream

    b. Foray

    c. Swamp

    d. Night

Part II Spatial Ability

1. When folded along the dotted lines, which shape will you get?

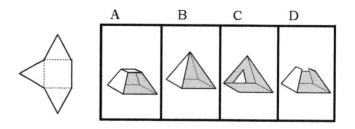

2. When folded, what pattern is possible?

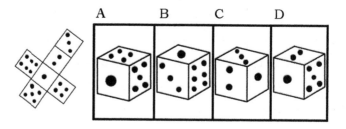

3. When folded into a loop, what will the strip of paper look like?

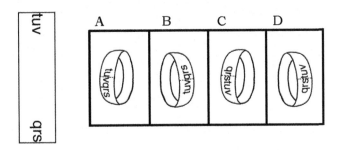

4. Which of the choices is the same pattern at a different angle?

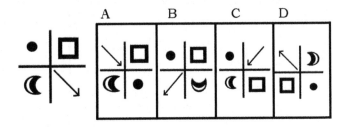

5. When put together, what 3-dimensional shape will you get?

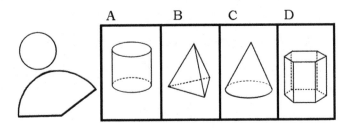

6. When folded, what pattern is possible?

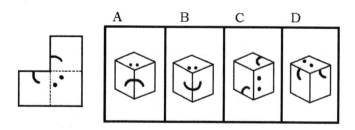

7. When folded, what pattern is possible?

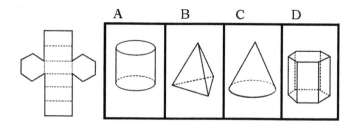

8. Which of the choices is the same pattern at a different angle?

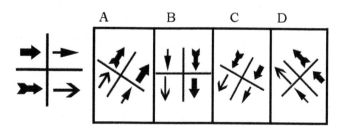

9. When put together, what 3-dimensional shape will you get?

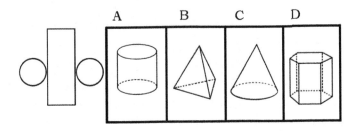

10. When folded into a loop, what will the strip of paper look like?

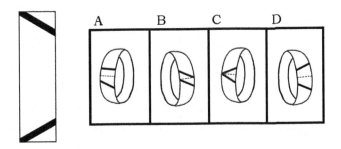

11. Which of the choices is the same pattern at a different angle?

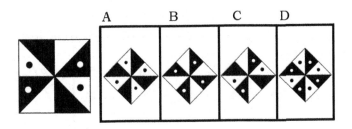

12. When put together, what 3-dimensional shape will you get?

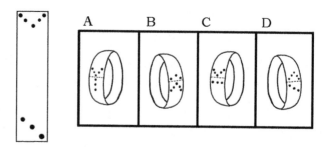

13. When folded into a loop, what will the strip of paper look like?

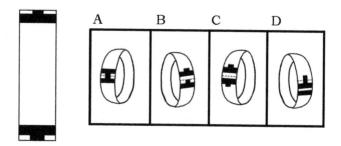

14. Which of the choices is the same pattern at a different angle?

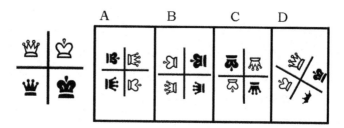

15. When folded into a loop, what will the strip of paper look like?

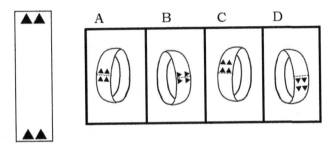

Part III - Problem Solving

1. A box is 15 cm long, 20 cm wide and 10 cm high. What is the volume of the box?

    a. 45 cm³

    b. 3,000 cm³

    c. 1500 cm³

    d. 300 cm³

2. Sarah weighs 25 pounds more than Tony. If together they weigh 205 pounds, what is Sarah's approximate weight in kilograms? Assume 1 pound = 0.4535 kilograms.

    a. 52

    b. 50

    c. 48

    d. 41

3. In a class of 83 students, 72 are present. What percent of student are absent? Provide answer up to two significant digits.

    a. 12

    b. 13

    c. 14

    d. 15

4. A store sells stereos for $545. If 15% of the cost was added to the price as value added tax, what was the cost before the tax?

    a. $490.40

    b. $473.90

    c. $575.00

    d. $593.15

5. Mr. Jones runs a factory. His total assets are $256,800 which consists of a building worth $80,500, machinery worth $125.000 and $51,300 cash. After one year what will be the total value of his assets if he has additional cash of $75,600 and the value of his building has increased by 10% per year, and his machinery depreciated by 20%?

    a. $243,450

    b. $252,450

    c. $264,150

    d. $272,350

6. Martin earns $25,000 basic pay, pays $500 rent and $860 medical allowance. He spends 40% of his total earning on food and clothing, 10% on children's education and pays $800 for utility bills. What percentage of his earning he is saving?

a. 44%

b. 47%

c. 50%

d. 54%

7. Prize money of $1,050 is to be shared among top three contestants in ratio of 7:5:3 as 1st 2nd and 3rd prizes respectively. How much more money will the 1st prize contestant get than the 3rd prize contestant?

a. $210

b. $280

c. $350

d. $490

8. The manager of a weaving factory estimates that if 10 machines run at 100% efficiency for 8 hours, they will produce 1450 meters of cloth. Due to some technical problems, 4 machines run of 95% efficiency and the remaining 6 at 90% efficiency. How many meters of cloth will these machines produce in 8 hours?

a. 1479 meters

b. 1310 meters

c. 1334 meters

d. 1285 meters

9.

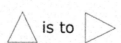

is to ⬡

△ is to ?

a. ▽   b. ◁

c. ▷   d. ⬭

10.

△ is to ▷

▢ is to ?

a. ▷   b. ☐

c. ⬠   d. ⬭

11.

▨ is to △

△ is to ?

a. △   b. ☐

c. ⬠   d. ▢

12.

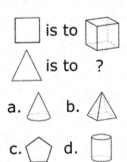

13.

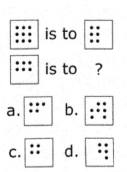

14.

15.

pentagon is to hexagon

hexagon is to ?

a. □   b. ◯

c. ⬠   d. ⬡

16.

circle is to ellipse

square is to ?

a. ▫   b. ▯

c. ▭   d. ◻

17. Consider the following sequence: ..., ..., 20, 32, 44, 56, 68. Find the first two terms.

    a. -4, 8
    b. 0, 12
    c. -6, 8
    d. 2, 8

18. Consider the following sequence: 3, 5, 10, 12, 24, ... What 2 numbers should come next?

    a. 48, 58

    b. 26, 28

    c. 48, 50

    d. 26, 52

19. Consider the following sequence: 1000, 992, 984, 976, ... What 2 numbers should come next?

    a. 968, 961

    b. 967, 960

    c. 968, 960

    d. 970, 964

20. Consider the following sequence: 0.1, 0.3, 0.9, 2.7, ... What 2 numbers should come next?

    a. -8.1, -24.3

    b. 8.1, 24.3

    c. 5.4, 10.8

    d. -5.4, -10.8

21. Consider the following sequence: 32, 16, 8, 4, ... What 3 numbers should come next?

    a. 2, 1, 0.5

    b. 2, 0,-2

    c. 0,-4,-8

    d. 2, 1, 0

22. Consider the following sequence: 3, ..., 9, 12, 15. What is the missing number?

    a. 4

    b. 7

    c. 6

    d. 5

23. Consider the following sequence: 1132, 1121, ... , 1199, ... What number comes next?

    a. 1109

    b. 1188

    c. 1189

    d. 1180

24. Consider the following sequence: 95, 90, ..., 80, 75. What is the missing number?

    a. 87

    b. 85

    c. 86

    d. 80

25. Consider the following sequence: ..., 75, 65, 60, 50, 45, 35, ... What 2 numbers are missing?

    a. 70, 35

    b. 65, 35

    c. 80, 30

    d. 65, 30

26. Consider the following sequence: 91, 85, ..., ..., 67, 61. What 2 numbers are missing?

    a. 81, 71

    b. 78, 72

    c. 80, 70

    d. 79, 73

27. Consider the following sequence: ..., ..., 120, 129, 138, 147. Find the first two terms.

    a. 102, 111

    b. 100, 110

    c. 102, 112

    d. 99, 111

28. Consider the following sequence: ..., 95, 88, 93, 86, 91, ... What 2 numbers are missing?

    a. 88, 98

    b. 90, 98

    c. 100, 84

    d. 90, 84

29. Consider the following sequence: 76, 64, 54, 46, ..., 36, ..., . What 2 numbers are missing?

    a. 40, 32

    b. 40, 34

    c. 42, 30

    d. 42, 32

30. Consider the following sequence: 3, ..., 12, ..., 48, 96. What 2 numbers are missing?

    a. 6, 36

    b. 6, 18

    c. 8, 16

    d. 6, 24

Answer Key

Part 1 - Verbal Skills

1. A
Jargon means the same as slang.

2. A
Render means the same as give.

3. B
Intrusive means the same as invasive.

4. A
Renown means the same as popular.

5. C
Incoherent means the same as jumbled.

6. A
Congenial means the same as pleasant.

7. A
Berate means the same as criticize.

8. B
Sate means the same as satisfy.

9. A
Abundant is the opposite of scarce.

10. C
Tough is the opposite of weak.

11. A
Simple is the opposite of complex.

12. B
Exhibit is the opposite of conceal.

13. D
Stingy is the opposite of generous.

14. B
Advance is the opposite of retreat.

15. D
Cease is the opposite of begin.

16. C
Immense is the opposite of tiny.

17. C
Redundant: Repetitive or needlessly wordy.

18. C
Bicker: To quarrel in a tiresome, insulting manner.

19. C
Sombre: Dark; gloomy.

20. A
Maverick: Showing independence in thoughts or actions, a rebel.

21. D
Tenuous: Thin in substance or consistency, weak.

22. A
Pandemonium: Chaos; tumultuous or lawless violence.

23. A
Perpetual: Continuing uninterrupted.

24. C
This is a process relationship. The first word is the process which creates the second. For example, ice melts to liquid in the same way water freezes to solid.

25. D
This is a measurement relationship. Clocks measure time in the same way thermometers measure temperature.

26. C
A car is kept in a garage the same way that a plane is kept in a hangar.

27. D
This is a place relationship. Acting is done in a theater in the same way gambling is done in a casino.

28. C
Pork is the meat of a pig in the same way beef is the meat of a cow.

29. A
This is a classification relationship. The first is the class to which the second belongs.

Fruit -> banana
Mammal -> rabbit

30. C
Slumber is a synonym for sleep and bog is a synonym for swamp.

Spatial Ability

1. B

2. A

3. D

4. D

5. C

6. B

7. D

8. C

9. A

10. C

11. C

12. D

13. A

14. B

15. A

Problem Solving

1. B
Formula for volume of a shape is L x W x H = 15 x 20 x 10 = 3,000 cm³

2. A
Let us denote Sarah's weight by "x." Then, since she weighs 25 pounds more than Tony, he will be x - 25. They together weigh 205 pounds which means that the sum of the two representations will be equal to 205:

Sarah : x

Tony : x - 25

x + (x - 25) = 205 ... by arranging this equation we have:

x + x - 25 = 205

2x - 25 = 205 ... we add 25 to each side to have the x term alone on one side:

2x - 25 + 25 = 205 + 25

2x = 230

x = 230/2

x = 115 pounds → Sarah weighs 115 pounds. Since 1 pound is 0.4535 kilograms, we need to multiply 115 by 0.4535 to have her weight in kilograms:

x = 115 * 0.4535 = 52.1525 kilograms → this is equal to 52 when rounded to the nearest whole number.

3. B
Number of absent students = 83 – 72 = 11

Percentage of absent students is found by proportioning the number of absent students to total number of students in the class = 11•100/83 = 13.25

Checking the answers, we round 13.25 to the nearest whole number: 13%

4. B
Actual cost = X, therefore, $545 = x + 0.15x$, $545 = 1x + 0.15x$, $545 = 1.15x$,
$x = 545/1.15 = \$473.9$

5. C
Cash = \$75600. Building after one year = $80500 \times 1.1 = \$88550$. Machinery after one year = $125000 \times 0.8 = \$100000$. Total asset value = \$264,150.

6. B
$25,000 - (500 + 860) = 23640$.
Food and clothing expense = $0.4 \times 23640 = 9456$
Education = $23640 \times 0.1 = 2364$
Utilities = 800
Total expenses = $9456 + 2364 + 800 = 12620$.
Amount of savings $23640 - 12620 = 11020$
$11020/23640 = X/100$
$X = 1102000/23640 = 46.6\%$ and round up to 47%.

7. B
The 1st prize winner will receive $7 \times 1050/15 = \$490$.
The 3rd prize winner will receive, $3 \times 1050/15 = \$210$.
The difference is $490 - 210 = \$280$.

8. D
At 100% efficiency 1 machine produces $1450/10 = 145$ m of cloth.

At 95% efficiency, 4 machines produce $4 *145 * 95/100 = 551$ m of cloth.

At 90% efficiency, 6 machines produce $6 * 145 * 90/100 = 783$ m of cloth.

Total cloth produced by all 10 machines = $551 + 783 = 1334$ m

Since the information provided, and the question are based on 8 hours, we did not need to use time to reach the answer.

9. A

The relation is the same figure rotated.

10. D

The relation is the same figure rotated.

11. B

The relation is a 3-dimensional figure to a 2-dimensional figure.

12. B

The relation is a 2-dimensional figure to a 3-dimensional figure.

13. C

The first figure has 9 dots in a square and the second figure has 6 dots, which is 1/3 removed.

14. C

The relation is a 3-dimensional figure to a rotated 2-dimensional figure.

15. B

The second figure contains more sides than the first.

16. B

The relation is the given figure to a horizontally compressed figure.

17. A

The sequence is increasing by 12. To find first two terms, we solve backwards by subtracting 12.

18. D

The sequence is increasing by adding 2 and multiplying 2 alternately. The next 2 terms are 24 + 2= 26 and
26 x 2 = 52.

19. C

The sequence is decreasing by 8.

20. B
The sequence is increasing by multiplying each the last term by 3. 2.7 x 3= 8.1 and 8.1 x 3 = 24.3

21. A
The sequence is decreasing by dividing the last term by 2.

22. C
The sequence is increasing by +3.

23. B
The sequence is reducing by 11.

24. B
The sequence is decreasing by +5.

25. C
The sequence is decreasing by -5 and -10 alternately; the first term is 75 – 5 = 70 and the last term is 35 – 10= 30.

26. D
The sequence is increasing by +6.

27. A
The sequence is increasing by +9.

28. D
The sequence is increasing and decreasing alternately. It increases by +5 and decreases by -7. The first term will thus be the second term 95 – 5 = 90 and the last term will be 91 – 7 = 84.

29. B
The difference between the terms starts from 12 and decreases by 2 i.e. 12, 10,8,6,4,2. The missing terms are 46 – 6=40 and 34 – 0 =34

30. D
Each term is being doubled or multiplied by 2 to get the next term. 3 x 2 = 6 and 12 x 2 = 24.

Conclusion

CONGRATULATIONS! You have made it this far because you have applied yourself diligently to practicing for the exam and no doubt improved your potential score considerably! Getting a good score on the CFAT is a huge step in a journey that might be challenging at times but will be many times more rewarding and fulfilling. That is why being prepared is so important.

Study then Practice and then Succeed!

Good Luck!

FREE Ebook Version

Download a FREE Ebook version of the publication!

Suitable for tablets, iPad, iPhone, or any smart phone.

Go to **http://tinyurl.com/nrn6krq**

Thanks!

If you enjoyed this book and would like to order additional copies for yourself or for friends, please check with your local bookstore, favourite online bookseller or visit www.test-preparation.ca and place your order directly with the publisher.

Feedback to the publisher may be sent by email to feedback@test-preparation.ca

Learn and Practice Proven multiple choice strategies!

If you are preparing for an exam, you probably want all the help you can get! You will learn:

- **Powerful multiple choice strategies** - Learn and then practice. Answer key for all practice questions with extensive commentary including tips, shortcuts and strategies.
- **How to prepare for a multiple choice exam** - make sure you are preparing properly and not wasting valuable study time!
- **Who does well on multiple choice exams** - and how to make sure you do!
- **How to handle trick questions** - usually there are one or two trick questions to separate the really good students from the rest - tips and strategies to handle these special questions.
- **Step-by-step strategy for answering multiple choice** - on *any* subject!

Also included:

- How to prepare for a test
- How to psych yourself up for a test
- How to take a test - What you *must* do in the test room
- Common mistakes on a test - and how to avoid them
- How to avoid anxiety

Remember it only a few percentage points divide the PASS from the FAIL students.

Why not do everything you can to increase your score?

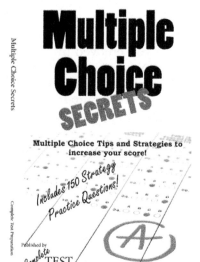

Multiple Choice Secrets

Complete Test Preparation

Multiple Choice Tips and Strategies to increase your score!

Includes 150 Strategy Practice Questions!

Published by
Complete TEST Preparation Inc.

Learn to increase your score using time-tested secrets for answering multiple choice questions!

This practice book has everything you need to know about answering multiple choice questions on a standardized test!

You will learn 12 strategies for answering multiple choice questions and then practice each strategy with over 45 reading comprehension multiple choice questions, with extensive commentary from exam experts!

Maybe you have read this kind of thing before, and maybe feel you don't need it, and you are not sure if you are going to buy this Book.

Remember though, it only a few percentage points divide the PASS from the FAIL students.

Even if our multiple choice strategies increase your score by a few percentage points, isn't that worth it?

Go to www.multiple-choice.ca
and get started today!